Money Ain't Free

❖

The True Cause of the Crisis in Corporate Responsibility

by Will Marshall

Author of Rich Shareowner,

Poor Shareowner! ™

iUniverse, Inc.

New York Lincoln Shanghai

Money Ain't Free
The True Cause of the Crisis in Corporate Responsibility

iUniverse, Inc.

For information address:
iUniverse, Inc.
2021 Pine Lake Road, Suite 100
Lincoln, NE 68512
www.iuniverse.com

ISBN: 0-595-29778-1

Printed in the United States of America

For

Marianne,

Emma, Fletcher, Rory,

and Selina

Contents

Acknowledgments

Thank you for buying *Money Ain't Free*. If you find merit in this book, please recommend it to others. After you read the book, I am sure that you will agree that it will take all of us working together to make the changes necessary to secure our children's economic future. Their economic freedom—the quality of jobs they have, the amount they can earn, and their economic choices—depends on making corporate America more effective in creating economic value (cash value) rather than just massaging accounting numbers.

This book and the positive actions it promotes are dedicated to future generations. However, the book would not have been published as a narrative had it not been for my mother. She is a gardener and homemaker who wouldn't normally read investment books. After breezing through the first draft twice in two days, she observed, "I like the way the conversational approach pulls me right through the book. I really understand this crisis now. When will it be fixed?" (Mother never had much patience with incompetence.)

I also want to especially thank my wife, Bev, and daughter, Marianne, for their encouragement over the years. Their support made it possible for me to learn, practice, and develop the ideas in this book.

Several other people deserve recognition, including Janet Van Der Bosch, who has provided me with great graphic designs, including my logo, website, and cover art.

From a professional standpoint, I have been greatly blessed with the friendship of many talented people at Nalco. I would especially like to recognize and thank Liz Ewing, Gerard Lemarche, Sergio Sousa, Steve Landsman, Gina Tuggle, Glen Haeflinger, Stan Gibson, Frederic Jung, Gilberto Pinzon, Craig Holderness, and Dave Blair. Their challenging questions and insights over the years have made me better both personally and professionally.

As a result of readers' actions, I trust that books in the *Rich Shareowner, Poor Shareowner!*™ series will contribute to strengthening free enterprise, and therefore economic freedom, for future generations.

Will Marshall

Hawthorn Woods, Illinois
December 2003

When something is "free",

it is usually abused.

Time,

Water,

Air,

Shareowners' Money.

Introduction

In 2001, questionable accounting and business practices at U.S. "energy giant" Enron, and the failure of its public accounting firm, Arthur Andersen, to report those practices to Shareowners, precipitated Enron's bankruptcy, Andersen's collapse, and a crisis of investor confidence in American business and the U.S. stock markets. The crisis became public before the September 11, 2001, terrorist attacks on America and coincided with a decline of over 50% in the Standard and Poors 500 stock index and almost 75% in the NASDAQ between September 2000 and October 2002. This represented a Shareowner loss of over $10 trillion dollars, an amount equal to approximately 1.5 times the national debt of the United States. This loss and the subsequent efforts to restore investor confidence in U.S. stocks are commonly known as the "crisis in corporate responsibility."

To date, the "root" cause of the crisis and its solution are publicly unknown.

<u>PART I</u>
The Call

1

Quiet Time

Sam McAllen snatched the phone from its cradle. He hated the way its shrill lament trespassed on the serenity of the ST Bar's high country lodge. Once the uninvited clamor ceased, however, he welcomed the voice at the other end of the line. It was the last week in November. Dude ranch guests had gone home and snow had begun to fall in Colorado's San Juan Mountains. Human contact had become scarce. It was almost too peaceful.

Sam's voice echoed from the lodge walls as he answered, "ST Bar Ranch. McAllen speaking."

From the other end of the line, he received an equally succinct reply. "New York calling. Stevens speaking."

Sam broke into a big grin and gave a hearty laugh as he said, "Helloooo, Wendy. How is my favorite investment-banking cowgirl?"

"Very well, Sam, and you?" came the warm response.

"I'm well," said Sam, "but I miss our talks and trail rides."

"I miss them too," Wendy said fondly.

As she continued, Sam detected a change in her voice. He sensed stress. "Sam, I need your help. Can we meet?"

"Of course," replied Sam. "I'll be in Chicago next Monday. Any chance of meeting there?"

"That works fine. I'll be in town with Sean calling on customers. Can you meet us at the Wildfire restaurant in Oak Brook Center at about 7 p.m.?"

"Done," replied Sam. "I know Wildfire well, and I look forward to seeing you and Sean again. But Wendy, give me a clue as to the type of help you need."

"Sam, my friends are confounded by what's happening in the stock market and with what the press is calling the 'crisis in corporate responsibility.' *Some people say the crisis is over. I know it's not.* My friends don't know who to believe or what to do. I want to give them good advice, but with so many things happening, I don't know where to begin."

"Sounds like you have some big concerns," said Sam.

"Yes," she replied, "especially since friends are involved; I feel so responsible to give them the best possible answer."

"Well, I think we can come up with some practical answers that'll do the job," he said.

"I know we will," she replied. Sam sensed the relief in her voice as she concluded. "See you in Chicago."

"Safe trip," he said as he hung up.

Sam looked down at the phone for a moment, smiled, then turned and ambled over to the lodge's huge fireplace. He tossed another log on the fire and sat down in his big leather rocking chair. It was dark outside. Dinner was over, and the day's chores were done.

Sam stared into the lively fire and sipped strong coffee from his old familiar mug. He smiled to himself.

This was thinking time.

PART II

Distractions

2

Wildfire

Sam arrived early at Oak Brook Center. He did so partly to allow time to negotiate the holiday crowds and partly to buy presents for special friends. However, deep down, Sam knew he had arrived early because he enjoyed being at the spectacular outdoor mall to stroll among the colorful, seasonal decorations, and to embrace the energy and enthusiasm of holiday shoppers. They added a different, but joyful, dimension to the quiet spiritual side of the holiday that he experienced in the Rockies. While he had been to Oak Brook Center to shop many times during his years as a corporate financial officer, Sam always marveled at how the center's size and charm grew between his visits.

At 6:30, Sam walked into the Wildfire restaurant and followed the hostess to the table reserved in Wendy's name. While he waited, he surveyed the large room, taking in the ambiance of polished wood and well-dressed patrons. He smiled as he contrasted it with the hewn log walls and rough dress of the wranglers at the ST Bar lodge. Flames dancing under steaks on the Wildfire's grill reminded him of the ranch campfires back home and how similar things were beneath even the most elegant veneer.

His reflections faded as he glanced up to see an attractive young couple walking toward the table. Wendy Stevens led the way. A poised, knowledgeable young woman in her mid-30s, Wendy had made her career in investment banking by helping companies issue debt and equity, as well as by guiding them toward their goals in corporate finance, in addition to mergers and acquisitions. Sam had to admit, Wendy's well-tailored pinstripe business suit was a far cry from the ranch clothes she had worn when they first met during her vacation at the ST Bar this past summer. In their short week together at the ranch, Wendy and Sam had developed respect for each other's common sense and character, and from that, the rapport of close friends.

With her was a young man in his early 20s. Sam had known him for about eight years, but they had spent so much time in jeans and chaps riding at the ranch that Sam hardly recognized Sean Lone Eagle in his investment-banker getup. Sean was at home on the range or on Wall Street. He had earned a mathematics degree at Cal Tech, and after working three years as an investment analyst on Wall Street, he had completed the first year of an MBA at Stanford. Sean was currently delaying the second year of his MBA in order to learn some "honest" investment banking from Wendy. Sean Lone Eagle was a Lakota Sioux and claimed to have taught Sam all that he knew about scouting. Over the years, he and Sam had traded lessons. Sean taught Sam how an Indian scout tracks, and Sam taught Sean corporate finance and how value is created by and for Shareowners. Each felt it was a fair trade.

Wendy greeted Sam with a big hug, saying, "It's wonderful to see you. Thanks for coming."

"It's my pleasure," he said.

Sam reached out to accept Sean's firm handshake. "Good to see you, Lone Eagle, my friend."

Sean smiled broadly. It was good to hear his tribal name again. "Likewise, Kemo Sabe. I hope you are taking care of the ST Bar horses as I taught you."

Sam grinned. "And I hope you're creating value for Shareowners as I taught you."

Sean nodded and held Wendy's chair as she sat down at the table. The three friends enjoyed small talk and banter until their drinks arrived. After a toast to friendship and shared experiences, Wendy became serious.

3

Wendy's Request

"Sam, I really appreciate your time, and I really need your help," said Wendy.

Sam nodded. "That's why I came."

Wendy smiled. "Thank you, Sam." Then she began her story. "My friends range from secretaries to CEOs and CFOs, but when they admit it, they all have a common problem. My friends are scared to invest in stock because they don't understand what is going on, whom to trust, or what to believe. The sad part is that they're not alone. Earlier this month, I read a *USA Today* poll that said over seventy percent of Americans making more than $75,000 didn't feel knowledgeable about when to buy or sell stock, and almost sixty-five percent didn't feel competent evaluating a company's financial statements before buying a stock.[1] Based upon the people that I know, these *USA Today* numbers are severely understated. My guess is that honest answers to the poll would have produced discomfort figures closer to ninety-five percent."

Sam nodded and said, "I'm sure you're right."

Wendy continued, "We had wonderful discussions at the ST Bar last summer.[2] They gave me terrific insights into how *both* Shareowners and managers create value for Shareowners, and how to determine a fair stock price for a company. But as helpful as those ideas have been, I need an even simpler technique that my friends can understand, something they can use every day to help them put cash in their pockets. Even if we can devise a simpler way to determine if a company's stock is over-or undervalued, we also need to restore my friends' confidence in stock by eliminating the distractions that are making them afraid to invest."

Sam frowned. "Is there anything else that might help your friends regain confidence?"

"There is," she replied, "but I don't know how to express it."

"Let me try," interjected Sean. "Wendy and I discussed this on the plane coming out here. I think that I can explain it by relating it to our tracking experiences at the ST Bar." He moved his drink and ran his finger through the wet ring it left on the tabletop, creating a meandering trail. "As you know, Sam, when a scout tracks a bear, he doesn't just look down at the ground and follow the tracks. Besides knowing it's a good way to get ambushed, a scout knows that he can never get ahead of, or into, the head of the bear by following its tracks. Instead, a good scout is constantly observing nature for things that are unusual. For example, if birds and deer flush from behind a hill, he knows something caused this unusual movement. Was it the bear? If so, the scout knows where the bear likely is, not just where the tracks show the bear had been. But even beyond that, as I taught you, Sam, a good scout tries to get inside the bear's head to figure out what motivates the animal. Is he tired, hungry, thirsty, or running from something? By knowing the lay of the land and what motivates the bear, the scout anticipates where the bear will be—often before the bear knows."

Sam nodded as Sean continued, "Wendy and I sense there is a larger issue out there that has not been publicly recognized. It's the real cause of this crisis of confidence in the capital markets. I think that the public senses this, and until we eliminate this unknown apparition, the public will not fully trust stock. It's like we are all waiting for the other shoe to drop. Sam, we need to identify this unknown issue if we are going to get inside the head of the bear and understand what's really causing this so-called crisis in corporate responsibility."

"I agree," said Wendy. "There is something else out there. And, like Sean, I'd like to understand it, so that my friends and I can anticipate how it will affect stock. We also want to know if the problem is being fixed."

Sam sat back and looked from Wendy to Sean, waiting for further comments. Both of them had become used to Sam's silent waiting technique. This time they conspired to wait him out.

After a few moments, Sam finally broke the silence. "Let me make sure that I understand what you need. You want to help your friends regain their confidence in stock and overcome needless fear caused by distractions?"

Wendy nodded. "Yes."

Sam continued, "And you also want a simple method that they can use by themselves to identify whether a stock is over-or undervalued?"

Wendy nodded again.

Sam turned to Sean. "And you, my friend, want insight into the real cause of the so-called crisis in corporate responsibility."

Wendy and Sean both nodded.

"Hmm." Sam paused, looking down at the table. "No small order."

He sat quietly for a minute, then turned to Sean and said, "You know that the media thinks corrupt corporate executives are the cause of this crisis and the politicians and prosecutors think that more regulation and jail time is the solution."

Sean nodded. "That's what you might expect from reporters and lawyers. They want quick, graphic solutions. And many of them believe that penalties change motivation. I guess sometimes if motivations are weak, penalties *can* change behavior. But in this case, these reporters and lawyers haven't discovered the true *power* or nature of the motivation causing this corporate crisis. The power behind this crisis isn't going to be tamed by a few strands of chicken wire being put up to prevent the bear from getting to the raw meat. We need a way to change the motivation of this bear toward a different goal."

Sam looked Sean in the eye, smiled, and said, "I agree. They haven't discovered that the real motivation behind this crisis is free enterprise. And in a free society, you can't legislate either morality or a change in what motivates people."

Sam sat back and smiled before continuing. "No, the politicians, lawyers, and press haven't learned that while penalties and regulations may deter people, they don't change people's goals. Motivating people toward new goals requires a much different solution than threatening them with penalties."

4

Distractions

After taking a long, slow pull of water, Sam smiled and said, "Wendy, it sounds to me like you want me to help your friends navigate between the excesses of fear and Greater Fools."

Wendy rolled her eyes, grinned, and whispered to Sean, "I knew he was going to get to that Greater Fool theory." Sean chuckled.

Sam ignored them and continued, "It's natural for your friends to fear the unknown. Let's see if we can help them by converting the unknown into the known." He leaned forward. "It's simple to explain how to overcome fear and extremes in the stock market. The solution involves two elements: learning to recognize a 'fair' stock valuation and learning to recognize and ignore distractions.

"The challenge for your friends will be to discipline themselves to ignore the distractions and to discipline themselves to invest based upon the real value of a company. They must stop investing based on the assumption that there will always be someone else to bail them out at a higher stock price."

"In other words," said Wendy, "they must discipline themselves to avoid investing based on what you and Sean call the Greater Fool Theory."

Sam smiled, nodded, and made a request. "Wendy, before we talk about a simpler method for determining the real value of a company, let's hear about some of the distractions that are scaring your friends. Perhaps we will see a pattern in them that will give your friends the ability to eliminate distractions so that they can focus and invest based on a stock's real value."

Sean raised his hand and interrupted. "Sam, before Wendy begins, let's make sure that we are on the same page. You have used the term 'real value' of a company several times. Please explain what you mean."

"Sure," replied Sam. "The real value of a company is the value of all the cash inside it. That includes all of its present and future cash."

"OK," said Sean. "Your definition of real value is what we usually call the Enterprise Value."

"Right," said Sam. "We should use that term in our conversation in order to avoid confusion."

Sam retrieved some paper from his canvas briefcase and spoke as he wrote. "To make sure that we are all reading from the same music, let's look at the following simple equation, which represents the value of all the cash in the company."

Enterprise Value	= Current Cash	- Current Debt	+ Present Value of All Future Free Cash Flow (Including Growth)

Sam continued, "The equation says that the Enterprise Value of a company equals—

1. Cash held in bank accounts or liquid investments, MINUS

2. Cash required to pay off *all* borrowed debt, PLUS

3. Current (present) value of all the cash that it will generate in the future and that can be returned to Shareowners without impairing growth.

"It is similar to saying that your personal Enterprise Value is equal to—

1. Cash that you have in your pocket and bank accounts, MINUS

2. Debt that you owe, PLUS

3. The current value (today's value) of all the cash that you will get in the future from either your work or from selling any assets that you currently own."

"Agreed," said Sean.

Wendy collected her thoughts as Sam turned the page on his pad of paper and prepared to scribble notes.

Wendy began. "Clearly the Enron/Anderson debacle has distracted and scared a lot of people. It was a cathartic event."

"A what?" teased Sean.

Sam pretended to make a note and asked, "How do you spell cathartic?"

Wendy laughed. "OK, you guys. Let me put it in a way so that even you two outlaws can understand. It was the straw that broke the pack mule's back."

"Ah," Sean said, grinning. "Now I'm with you. Please continue."

Wendy raised an eyebrow and pretended to watch him warily from the corner of her eye as she continued. "The Enron/Andersen debacle didn't cause the crisis in corporate responsibility. However, Enron/Andersen became the catalyst that focused public attention on the failure of companies to govern themselves in their Shareowners' interests. These governance failures in a few companies grew into *three key distractions* that many ascribed to all companies."

Sam noted her three distractions:

- Lack of faithfulness of Enron's financial reporting to generally accepted accounting principles (GAAP)
- Failure of the Andersen auditors to report Enron's lack of faithfulness to GAAP
- Fraud committed by some Enron managers

"Why are these distractions?" asked Sam.

"Well," said Wendy, "all three issues are real problems. But, the frenzy surrounding accusations of fraud in a small minority of companies such as Enron, WorldCom, Tyco International, Adelphia Communications, and Global Crossing has grown to the point where all companies have been unfairly painted with the same doubts. As a result, we are in a "witch-hunting" mode. Sensational headlines are distracting all of us from looking for the real cause of the crisis of confidence in our financial markets."

"Interesting comment," mused Sam. "What's been the response to these Enron/Andersen distractions?"

"First, as you know, the Justice Department prosecuted the Andersen accounting firm for failing to provide proper audits. Andersen was found guilty and is no longer in the accounting business," replied Wendy.

"That should have sent a clear message to other accounting firms," said Sam, "but it also should have sent a message to the public that the prosecutors and regulators were now on a heightened alert and that penalties for accountants who fail in their duties to investors could be severe. As a result, there should be much less risk of auditors failing to do their job of ensuring accuracy of company financials and conformance to generally accepted accounting principles."

"Right," Wendy continued, "and further supporting your conclusion is that in 2002, Congress passed the Sarbanes-Oxley Act, which, among other safeguards, established the Public Company Accounting Oversight Board within the Securities and Exchange Commission (SEC) to set auditing standards and monitor the auditors' performance—to 'audit the auditors,' so to speak."

"So, a clear message has been sent to auditors about the severe consequences of failed audits. In addition, new professional oversight has been established on the accounting profession to help prevent failed audits," said Sam. "Our government is at work protecting us."

Wendy suspiciously eyeballed Sam as she poured some balsamic vinegar on her salad. After a moment she said, "I assume that your sarcasm relates to the fact that while Harvey Pitt was chairman of the SEC, he acted like the ring master of a flying circus. As a result, implementing the Public Company Accounting Oversight Board within the SEC—to 'audit the auditors'—has been a surrealistic, long, and painful experience for the financial markets and our country."

"That's part of it," replied Sam. "It was clear then, and is clear now, that Pitt and others, including the economic advisors to several recent presidents as well as Federal Reserve Board ('Fed') Chairman Alan Greenspan, were out of their element and unable to determine the real cause of the crisis. As a result, instead of getting ahead of the problem, they were constantly trying to catch up."

Sam wanted to refocus on the topic at hand, so he offered a temporary conclusion. "The government bureaucracy is surely both a distraction and a tragic comedy that we need to talk about. But first, let's go back and discuss what has been done in response to the Enron/Andersen debacle to ensure that companies and corporate officers are more accountable for reporting their GAAP financials honestly to the Shareowners."

Sean responded, giving Wendy a chance to take a bite of her salad, "The SEC issued new regulations requiring that audit committees of companies include outside 'independent' directors. The SEC also required the CEO and CFO to certify to the accuracy of their company's financial statements under oath. Failure to comply exposes them to criminal penalties. The Justice Department and various state attorneys general also began to intensify prosecution of individual officers and accountants at various organizations that had broken the law and defrauded investors. Companies like Andersen, WorldCom, Enron, Adelphia, and Tyco come to mind. Politicians, prosecutors, regulators, law enforcement officials, and the media have had a field day printing perp walks on the front pages."

Wendy put down her fork and showed obvious disapproval. "While we have to enforce the law, I disagree with the 'pop-perp' law-enforcement methods that were used. It may have been a way to get headlines in an attempt to deter others, but I wonder whether the politicians, as well as the prosecutors, regulators, and law-enforcement officials, didn't violate the rights of the accused. When many of the accused prearranged to voluntarily turn themselves in, they were slapped in handcuffs and displayed to the press like trophies. They hadn't been convicted. A handcuff parade for the benefit of the press and to get headlines, is character assassination. From the standpoint of future employment in the financial world, it is the equivalent of a death sentence *even* if the accused is later found innocent. *Even* if we give prosecutors the benefit of the doubt and assume that their objective with the handcuff parade was to provide a visible deterrent to others, their ends don't justify the means. In this country, people are presumed innocent until judged guilty in court of law by a jury of peers. Prosecutors don't have the prerogative to preempt or to unilaterally repeal that right. Frankly, the perp walks struck me as a publicity grab by prosecutors rather than good law enforcement."

Sean grimaced and added, "Frankly, Wendy, the prosecutors' public displays created an even bigger distraction for your friends."

"How so?"

"My guess is that these public parades created unnecessary investor fear, because the constant headlines and recurring pictures of perp walks made the problem seem more extensive than it really was. It also distracted people into thinking that the primary cause of the crisis was dishonest executives. The perp walks have given the public a false sense of security by lulling them into complacency. While there are a few executives who are criminals, executives are not the real cause of the problem. In fact, as I said earlier this evening, I don't think that the root cause of the problem has been publicly identified, or we wouldn't be having this conversation. If the root cause had been identified and corrected, the public would be convinced that the crisis was over and be comfortable buying stocks. They aren't."

Wendy nodded in frustrated agreement. The three of them sat in silence for a few moments.

Finally, Sam restored direction to the conversation. "There are many difficult issues and many *vested interests* swirling around this crisis of confidence in the capital markets. It's clear that the politicians—prosecutors included—and law-enforcement officials have taken liberties at the expense of principles that they are sworn to protect. Time will be the judge as to whether their actions were simply poor judgment or political theater to enhance their personal political agendas."

"You're right. Let's continue," Wendy said in a subdued voice.

Sam looked at her. "Wendy, a few minutes ago, you said that it felt like we were on a witch-hunt, and that these three distractions were preventing us from identifying the real cause of our lost confidence in the financial markets. Why do you think that?"

Wendy looked at Sam as she responded. "I recently read that the Government Accounting Office reported that, since 1997—over approximately the past five years—only ten percent of public companies had to restate their financials.[3] And of those, only a very small minority had committed fraud as opposed to those who had made honest mistakes. After all, generally accepted accounting principles leave a reasonable degree of room for ambiguity and interpretation because of the variety of industries and circumstances that they have to account for. But, in spite of all the adverse publicity surrounding financial reporting at companies like Enron, WorldCom, Global Crossing, Adelphia, and Tyco, an objective observer has to conclude that financial information in the U.S. is reliably reported in accordance with GAAP. The dishonesty in a few companies like Enron is distracting, but is not indicative of corporate America in general. While it is popular to think that unfaithful financials and crooked corporate officers are the cause of the crisis in corporate responsibility, the data does not support a conclusion of mass infidelity or even of extensive infidelity to GAAP. *So, I conclude that infidelity to GAAP is NOT the cause of the crisis of confidence in capital markets.*"

"Good insight," Sam said. "There is another logical conclusion to be drawn from the GAO data that you mentioned. *If ninety percent of the companies reported their financials in accordance with GAAP, then false financial reporting doesn't account for, and isn't the cause of, the excessive valuations that caused the dot-com, telecom, or stock-market bubbles of the 90s.* After all, it wasn't the companies that ran their price-to-earnings (P/E) multiples to historic levels, in many cases to multiples well in excess of 100. Someone else did that."

"You're right. But *who*?" Wendy questioned. "Those market bubbles are the biggest part of the reason that my friends are so scared of stocks."

Sean seized the opportunity for a little fun and emitted a ghostly "*Whooooo? Whooooo? Whooooo?*"

After a brief pause, the ghostly response came from the other side of his mouth, "*Greater Fools…*"

"Okay, okay. Have your fun," said an animated Wendy as she glowered at Sean. "Get me off the hot seat here. If you are so *wise*, tell us about the next distraction. How about one that explains why the stock prices ran up so much?"

Brokers

With some effort Sean recovered his composure and volunteered an answer: "Brokers."

Sam asked, "Why are brokers a distraction to investors, and how do they cause excessive valuations?"

"Brokers speak with forked motivation," said Sean.

Now it was Wendy's turn. "Whoa," she said, laughing. "Tell me the truth. Are you trying to get back at me for my 'cathartic pack mule' remark? Is 'forked motivation' part of a secret-code language that you and Sam speak when you're out on the range?"

"No," laughed Sean "and I am *not* saying that brokers speak with forked tongue.

What I mean is that brokers are hard-working people, but they have multiple loyalties. These multiple loyalties result in many conflicting interests tugging on them. Therefore, as a *practical* matter, an investor can never be sure if his broker is giving advice in the investor's interest, or if the broker is giving the advice primarily because there is something in it for the broker. Even if the individual broker can put aside all the conflicts and give advice purely to help the investor, the potential for conflict is so obvious that the investor can never be sure."

"Are you one of those people that says, 'Never trust a broker'?" asked Wendy.

"No," said Sean. "I'm saying that *knowledgeable investors understand the motivation of people around their money.* In the case of brokers, knowledgeable investors will always have questions about the motivation behind a trade recommendation. Therefore, the prudent investor will make sure that he does some basic homework before acting on a broker's recommendation."

Sam picked up on the conversation and turned to Wendy. "There are several important insights to be gained from this distraction that will give your friends the ability to eliminate other distractions.

"The first insight is that *free enterprise is a process in which each individual acts in his own self-interest, and in the process creates value for society.* Adam Smith explained how value was created for society through the division of labor in his classic work, *Wealth of Nations,* written in 1776.

"The point of this first insight is that *acting in one's self-interest is fundamental to our society. Every adult—especially Shareowners—should expect it of others and act accordingly.* After all, the Shareowner himself is acting in his self-interest; in the process, his capital creates products and jobs that people need and want. However, we need to differentiate between someone acting in his self-interest and someone acting in his own selfish self-interest."

"Explain," commanded Wendy.

Sam responded, "If someone commits fraud—a crime—then they are acting in their own *selfish* self-interest. In fact, there is a gray area where someone in a fiduciary role, such as a corporate officer, can act in his *selfish* self-interest, and it is not a crime. There will always be gray areas where good judgment and character are required. However, *acting in one's own self-interest is not a crime.* In a free society, it would be naive to think otherwise. Investors need to accept this reality and deal with it. *Knowledgeable investors deal with it before the fact, i.e. before they invest, because they know that after the fact, even an army of lawyers can't recover enough to compensate all the plaintiffs of a bankrupt or restructured company.* We accept this reality of self-interest when we are buying a car from a used car salesman. We need to deal with the distractions and people surrounding stock and other investments in the same way."

Sam continued, "The second lesson to be learned from this 'distraction' is that by identifying how a person is measured and paid, i.e. motivated, you can usually extrapolate what he or she will do, and why.

"For example, the broker, *and* the brokerage company he works for, earns money when they buy or sell stock or bonds—corporate debt—for a customer. They earn even more money if they are selling the stock or bonds of a company that has hired them to issue new stock or debt for it. The reason is that the company is also paying the brokerage company, or its affiliated investment bank, a fee for the same trade. The self-interest of the broker and the brokerage is turnover, *not* how well the customer's portfolio performs."

"But if the broker and the brokerage don't look out for the customer's portfolio and best interests in the long run, won't they go out of business?" Wendy asked.

"Brokerage advertising would lead you to believe that. It is very customer friendly," said Sam. "But that's the pretty face. It's skin deep. Industries and companies have their own cultures, just like nations. The true culture of these brokerages is very different from the public persona. And it is the culture of the industry and company that influences how their employees deal with customers."

Sam continued, "The reality is that no brokerage has a dominant share of the very large investor market. And, except for the rare individual, most managers in the financial services industry are very near term, 'bottom-line'-focused and have adopted a corporate culture that takes for granted that there are plenty of customers out there. If they lose a customer, they believe that they can get two others.

This brokerage culture is reinforced by measurement, incentive pay, and job security based on volume and turnover. Therefore, their focus is on the fees that a customer can generate for 'me' *this* year. This attitude permeates the culture of firms associated with Wall Street, and consequently, individuals in the firms become focused on keeping their jobs and their own current-year incentives as a matter of survival. From their perspective, there is nothing wrong with this focus. It's a reality. Investors just have to accept it and deal with these salespeople in this context. Brokers' economic interests are not the same as yours. *The key is to understand this and for your friends to use their brokers rather than letting the brokers use them."*

Wendy said, "Some of my friends would ask if your observation is true of brokers and firms that charge annual fees as a percent of total assets—in other words, 'performance-based' fees,"

"Good question," Sam responded. "Performance-based fees do not change the fact that brokers and brokerages may still be earning big fees from the companies who are trying to issue new stocks or bonds. Therefore, the brokerage or brokers may be willing to temporarily hold or 'park' the issuing company's new stock or bond in the investor's performance-based portfolio.[4] There are many other transactions that brokerages and mutual funds can do that earn fees for them at the expense of Shareowners.[5] But aside from that, the concept of performance fees is flawed unless the fee is only paid on the amount by which the portfolio performance exceeds some passive, benchmark index—for example, the Standard & Poors 500 stock index—over, say, a three-year performance period. If a broker or mutual-fund manager can't produce premium performance to the index, then there should be no more fees than needed to cover index maintenance. Performance-based fees make an excellent marketing story, but in reality, they let brokers earn fees as a percent of assets even when there is no turnover in the portfolio or when the portfolio underperforms against the benchmark.

"In any event," observed Sean, "the fact that there are fewer or no fees doesn't restore an investor's lost money or lost opportunity resulting from poor performance. The old saying applies: 'There is no free lunch on Wall Street.'"

Sam nodded agreement and concluded, "Let me repeat the two general guidelines when it comes to people and money."

Wendy noted on her pad:

- *You must assume that everyone is acting in his own self-interest.*
- *You can usually predict what a person will do and what his self-interest is, if you can identify how he and his company are measured and paid.*

She nodded thoughtfully. "While at first that may seem like a very callous attitude, it's logical. And I will admit that it's true in my experience. It's important that we all approach investing with the attitude of *caveat emptor*—let the buyer beware."

Sam smiled and nodded. "A classic idea, immortalized by the Romans."

Then Wendy asked, "But Sam, when are you going to give my friends that benchmark of a stock's value so that they know when to buy or sell?"

"Patience," he replied.

Their steaks arrived and Wendy made a note. She pushed on with some reluctance. "That leads us to my next distraction: investment analysts."

Investment Analysts

Sam grinned and sat back as he watched their entrees being served. "OK, Sean, you've worked as a junior investment analyst. How is the profession a distraction?"

Sean looked longingly at his steak. "You're trying to ruin my dinner, aren't you?"

Wendy and Sam laughed while Sean cut off a piece of steak and ate it before they finished laughing and made him answer.

After a second bite, he reluctantly took up the question. "If I think about investment analysts in terms of how they are measured and paid, I can only conclude that their best interest is to generate business for the investment bank or brokerage for which they work. It's the investment bank or brokerage that pays them. Most often, the investment bank and brokerage are owned by the same public company."

Sean paused in thought, and then continued, "An investment analyst's loyalty to the investing public or to the company issuing stocks or bonds is limited. It's limited to the amount of fees that the individual customer generates for his bank or brokerage, either by buying or selling something through the brokerage or by making it possible for the investment bank to earn fees from a company."

"Elaborate," challenged Sam.

Sean nodded, grabbed another bite, and responded. "Investment analysts work for investment banks and brokerage firms. The investment banks earn multimillion-dollar fees from corporate customers when they provide mergers and acquisitions (M&A) advice, conduct share repurchases, provide corporate finance products, or raise new debt or equity for a company as in IPOs (Initial Public Offerings). Investment banks also earn money on stock or bonds traded through their brokerage subsidiaries. The simple act of an investment banker inviting an analyst to join him on a visit to a company's CEO or CFO does two things. It reminds the investment analyst of the business that the investment banker is trying to win from the company, and it reminds the CEO and CFO of the fact that the investment bank's analyst is rating their company. Implicitly, there is the possibility that the investment bank will stop having the analyst 'follow' or 'rate' the company if the investment bank doesn't get enough corporate business."

Wendy nodded. "That's true. I remember when I was in training as a junior investment banker. We'd been calling on a corporate customer for a number of years, trying to get him to do some acquisitions and use our investment bank as the advisor. One day, my managing director decided to take the equity analyst who followed the company with us to visit the CEO and CFO. At the meeting the investment analyst told the CEO that the company was almost too small for him to follow, since big mutual funds needed bigger companies with larger market capitalization and better liquidity in order to accommodate their large investments. The next day, my boss got a call from the CFO adding us to their list of M&A advisors and asking us to bring them some deals. As a postscript, our analyst had been following many companies half the size of this particular customer for years and hadn't dropped them."

Wendy changed direction with a question. "Sam, let's talk about the impact on my friends, who want to buy and sell stock based on analysts' recommendations. Some of them are still puzzled. Why there are so many buys issued even when stock markets are overvalued and have started to fall, and even when individual stocks have fallen over fifty percent?"

Sam said, "Well, let's go back to understanding the source of job security, measurement and pay for investment analysts and their investment banks and/or brokerages."

Sam continued speaking so that Sean and Wendy could eat. "First of all, analysts work for Wall Street firms, which, as we have discussed, are *not* charitable institutions. These firms earn billions of dollars annually from companies who pay them for merger-and-acquisition advice, corporate finance products, and issuance of debt and equity. The Wall Street firms don't want to alienate client companies' CEOs by putting sell recommendations on their stock. If they alienate the CEOs, the companies will not hire them for these other profitable services. In addition, analysts like to recommend companies that are 'growing.' Usually, analysts don't define or are ambiguous as to what has to grow, such as sales, earnings, and cash flow. As a result, it leaves the door open for investment bankers to put pressure on company managers to 'grow' through acquisitions. Unfortunately, as we discussed at the ranch last summer, studies have determined that seventy to eighty percent of acquisitions are the wrong source of 'growth,' because companies overpay and destroy Enterprise Value by diluting the return on Shareowner's capital. As a result, their stock price growth, earnings growth, cash flow growth, and other operating ratios *underperform* peers over two-to five-year periods following the material acquisitions."[6]

"The second reason that analysts don't like to put sell recommendations on stocks is that Wall Street brokerages make fees from individual investors through brokerage transactions. Now, if analysts are constantly recommending buys, not only does the price of the stock on which the fee may be based have an upward bias, but also, the fully invested investor has to sell something in order to buy the new recommendation. That's two trades (a sell and a buy) and two commissions. On the other hand, if most recommendations are sell, then the investor just sells—one trade—and is probably scared to reinvest if the majority of other recommendations are sell. Brokerage fees dry up as well as corporate business."

Sam continued, "Like any employee, investment analysts hold their jobs—a few earning as much as $5 to $20 million a year—at the discretion of the CEO of the Wall Street firm. As a result, even if there were 'firewalls' or 'Chinese walls' between the investment analysts and the investment bankers so that analyst pay did not depend directly on the performance of the investment bank, the firewalls wouldn't work. There will always be some component of analyst compensation, whether in the form of bonuses, profit sharing, stock options, or stock ownership, which is based on the profitability of the firm. All of these, as in any company, are ultimately at the discretion of the investment bank's CEO. Therefore, it's impossible to eliminate this natural conflict."

"That's pretty Machiavellian, Sam," said Wendy. "Are you sure that you are not being a little mean-spirited?"

"Fair question, Wendy," Sam replied, nodding. "The facts speak for themselves. Most of Wall Street's products are commodity products, which are difficult to differentiate except on price. For example, a share of IBM stock is the same at Merrill Lynch as at Fidelity or Solomon Brothers. As a result, Wall Street firms live in a very 'dog-eat-dog' culture. Wall Street firms have two functions: to provide liquidity in financial markets and to make a profit for themselves. There is nothing in that culture about creating a profit for customers—if it happens, that's a byproduct. Let's also reflect on the fact that *Wall Street does not create economic value for our economy*—except a little at the extreme margin if they earn more than their Shareowners' cost of capital. *'Main Street' creates the economic value. Wall Street merely facilitates wealth transfer among people; in other words, it provides 'liquidity.'* This is a critical function, but, again, it is only a marginal creator of economic value for society. As such, from Wall Street's perspective, there is a winner for every loser, and Wall Street firms can always earn fees from the new winner—and often even from the loser. From the Shareowner's perspective, the efficiency of the wealth transfer depends on the size of the fees charged by Wall Street compared to the net wealth transferred to the Shareowner."

"But," Wendy interjected, "if Wall Street makes more money from both companies and brokerage clients when analysts issue buys, why are we beginning to see more sell recommendations from analysts? How do you explain that?"

"As an industry, Wall Street is as politically astute and connected as they come. Right now, they see that investors have temporarily backed away from overvalued markets and that prosecutors, regulators, and the media are after them. So, since money is not flowing into the market, they will give analysts a freer reign to issue sell signals. A few more sell signals are politically correct. It is also fascinating to observe the group-think among analysts, which demonstrates a certain self-preservation ethic. The sell or buy recommendations are rarely isolated occurrences, which raises another question. If analysts typically issue ratings within a notch of one another at virtually the same time, how does it benefit the investor, and why there are so many analysts on Wall Street?"

"There is only one answer to the second question," said Sean. "There are so many *analysts* because they *are there to help their investment banking or brokerage firm earn fees* from corporate and individual brokerage clients."

Sam nodded. "Related to that, there may also be another reason for the sell recommendations right now. Many of the stocks, whose prices are rated sell, have declined in price, and the sell rating causes Shareowners and creditors to put even more pressure on the company to restructure. This helps the investment bankers earn restructuring fees from companies without making the investment banker appear to be the advocate. As you know, restructuring, including divestitures, creates new fee opportunities for the investment banks, who may have just three to five years ago earned fees from the same companies by advocating the acquisition of the same businesses that must now be divested."

Sean said, "Right. Look at Vivendi International and AOL Time Warner. The French company Vivendi 'grew' by investing billions of dollars in acquisitions such as Universal Studios. AOL 'grew' by acquiring Time Warner, which in turn had borrowed billions to acquire other companies before it was acquired by AOL. While they grew in sales, and while executive paychecks got bigger, Shareowner value didn't grow—in fact, it shrank. Within four years of their principal acquisitions, both Vivendi and AOL Time Warner stock plunged over eighty percent, and both were forced to sell off parts of their acquired companies in order to pay off acquisition debt. Investment bankers made tens of millions in fees both during the acquisition and divestiture stages."

Wendy nodded, adding, "Yes, in every business cycle, I help some companies to divest what I helped them to acquire just a few years earlier. It is very sad to watch CEOs, CFOs, and directors make poor decisions that you know will have to be unwound later."

"I agree," Sam said, "and we'll discuss that later as part of the solution you will offer to your friends."

"Wendy, wait a minute," Sean interjected. "If you know that these CEOs and CFOs are making poor decisions, decisions that destroy value for Shareowners and that will have to be unwound, then why do you want to be an investment banker?"

"The CEOs have been influenced by others to do deals, and by the time that I become involved, the deals have a life of their own," she said. "While I try to persuade these CEOs and CFOs as to the proper way to look at the deals, sometimes they are so focused on their own GAAP-based incentive plans, or on hiding their failure to 'grow' the company, that there is nothing I can do. Nothing, except to ensure that the deal that they do is as favorable as possible to their company's Shareowners," she replied.

Sean lowered his head and nodded. From a personal perspective as a 'temporary' investment banker, he didn't appear happy about the answer.

Then Wendy played devil's advocate and said, "Some of my friends would suggest that the way to solve the conflict between the analysts' pay and their loyalties would be to legislate that they be employed by companies doing only independent research. In that way, investment banks can buy and provide investors with independent research alongside their own. How do you respond to that, Sam?"

"*Remember to follow the money*," replied Sam. "How are the independent research firms to be funded? If funding comes from the purchase of investment research by Wall Street, isn't Wall Street going to purchase the research that supports their own analysts' and, therefore, the investment bank's opportunities to earn fees? Even if Wall Street is forced to subsidize research, isn't Wall Street still going to be selective about which research they pass along to their clients? Either alternative will eventually influence the output of the 'independent' researchers."

Sam continued, "Look at another group of firms that were supposed to be independent and accountable to the investor, the auditors. In the end Arthur Andersen was killed by the aggressive pursuit of audit and consulting fees that resulted in failed audits at a variety of companies. Much of the current spate of corporate financial restatements results from auditors' failure to require strict compliance to GAAP. The auditors are lenient so that they can retain the client's auditing and consulting fees. What would make independent analytical firms immune to the same human frailties as auditors?"

"I see your logic," Wendy said, nodding.

Sean added a new insight. "The loyalties of financial analysts are becoming even more divided. To cut back on expenses, Wall Street firms are reducing research coverage of companies. As they do, some Wall Street firms are offering to provide research on companies, if the companies will pay for it.[7] Besides the issues mentioned by Sam, company-sponsored research raises the specter of companies shopping on Wall Street to buy the most favorable research opinions and recommendations."

"Wow," said Wendy. "When things change constantly and so quickly, who can Shareowners trust?"

Sam hit the table several times with the tip of his index finger to emphasize his next point. *"The biggest disservice to the public is to give them a false sense of security.* We shouldn't pretend to create firewalls or safety nets where it is logically impossible for them to exist. Instead, we need to make Shareowners aware of issues so that they can deal with them knowledgeably and objectively before problems arise. Let me remind you of another example of how numerous—dare I say ubiquitous—the routes to influence are. You've read about this example in the national papers. Many influential financial analysts live in greater New York. They want their children to go to the 'best' schools, even at the kindergarten level, because often these are perceived as the routes to the 'best' colleges. To get their children into these kindergartens, they sometimes need, or perceive that they need, influential people to make calls on their children's behalf, people such as their CEO or a lead investment banker.[8] When it comes to their family's well-being versus the investors' interests, it is impossible to know what seemingly innocent tradeoffs occur that put the investor last. This same logic can as easily apply to membership in country clubs, social clubs, sailing clubs, and so on."

Sam concluded, "In the end, it is impossible to insulate or regulate this type of human activity without infringing on the legitimate rights of citizens. However, we can educate. *If we give Shareowners the tools for thinking about the natural conflicts that exist when they invest, then they can act accordingly in their own self-interests. Forewarned is forearmed."*

There was a pensive silence at the table. Sam broke it. "Perhaps we should anticipate another question that Wendy's friends may ask. Why do some companies—such as Best Buy, with about $7.5 billion in market value; and General

Electric, with about $230 billion in market value—have twenty-two analysts rating them, but other companies with market caps of $2 billion to $30 billion have only one to eight analysts following them?"

Wendy responded, "I have often wondered about that. I suspect that if we were to calculate the total amount of investment banking business available from a client, and the volume of turnover in the client's stock, there would be a high correlation between a company's fee potential and the number of analysts following the company."

She continued, "What other logical reason can there be for twenty-two analysts to follow companies like Best Buy when there are no analysts following forty-four percent of the 3,800 companies in the Nasdaq Stock Market?[9] All this duplication is a tremendous waste of money, which adds no value to the investing public and can be rationally explained only in terms of the potential to add profits to the investment banks sponsoring the analysts. In fact, other than a grasp by investment banks for corporate business, how else can you explain how so many analysts missed a sell call on the dot-coms, telecoms, Enron, Quest, or World-Com?"

Wendy concluded, "In addition, the mere fact that there are so many analysts following any company creates another distraction for my friends. What is an investor to do when twenty-two analysts following a single $7.5-billion company render five 'strong buys,' eight 'moderate buys,' and nine 'holds'? Especially, when most of these same analysts never rated the stock a sell as it fell by over fifty percent in the preceding twelve months."

Sam replied, "The real answer is to be aware of analysts' recommendations. The 'announcement effect' of changes in their recommendations can precipitate a change in stock price. You should base your investment decision on how the stock's current market price compares to the Enterprise Value of the company. We discussed this at the ranch, but we will simplify those insights a little later."

Wendy directed another question to Sean. "Sean, how good are analysts' recommendations?"

Sean responded, "A number of studies have been done, including a recent one by New York's attorney general.[10] Some say the answers are inconclusive, even from those named to *Institutional Investor* magazine's 'All-America Research Team.' Other studies demonstrate that analysts' most-recommended stocks materially underperform their least-recommended stocks.[11] *However, the fact that some of the results are inconclusive reinforces the fact that analysts' recommendations are not very good.*"

"Why's that?" challenged Wendy.

"Well," said Sean, "analysts' results have been judged inconclusive *even after* they have benefited from things that should have improved their performance. For example, before they make their recommendations, they have historically been privy to 'earnings guidance' from the companies that they follow. The rest of us don't get that. In addition, the analysts' performance is judged *after* the stock price benefits from the 'announcement effect' of their own buy or sell recommendation."

"Good point," observed Wendy. "At least earnings guidance is no longer legal."

"Yes," said Sean, "but any good analyst knows how to read a CEO's body language—even over the phone."

Sam's eyes twinkled as he laughed to himself.

"What's worse," continued Sean, "I've seen some ad-hoc data showing that more than fifty percent of the time, analysts don't even rate companies a sell on the day the companies file for bankruptcy. On the day Global Crossing filed for bankruptcy, it had five buys, nine holds, and no sells."[12]

Wendy frowned as she nodded. "Yes, investment bankers can earn tens of millions of dollars in fees by helping a company to restructure in bankruptcy, so you can understand why investment analysts may be reluctant to recommend a sell even at bankruptcy."

"You know," she continued, "in keeping with your observation on analysts' performance, it is fascinating to me that a number of well-known analysts are leaving the business. While some of them say that it is because their recommendations are increasingly subject to bureaucratic scrutiny, I wonder if the smart ones realize that even when you consider things like earnings guidance and announcement effects, their recommendations didn't outperform even in the rising markets of the 90s. Now that markets are moving sideways, falling, or have become real stock pickers' markets, analysts' failure to add value will be even more obvious to the public. The smart investment analysts recognize that the easy money has been made."

They ate in silence, digesting everything that had been said.

Finally, Sean spoke. "Do you know what has troubled me most about the investment analyst position, and what caused me to leave Wall Street to work on my MBA—except for this chance to learn some investment banking from Wendy?"

"What's that?" inquired Sam.

"*I cannot identify a scenario in which investment-analyst recommendations make sense for the investing public,*" replied Sean.

"Think about it," he continued. "Even if you knew which of the twenty-two analysts to believe, and even if you could eliminate conflicts and suspicions of conflicts, a stock's price often moves ten percent or more within an hour or two following a ratings change by an analyst, and may move twenty-five percent or more within forty-eight hours if the market becomes concerned about the stock."

"And your point?" asked Wendy.

"Well," replied Sean. "Who does the analyst call first with the ratings change?"

Wendy was ready with the answer, "Obviously, the first call is to the customers who generate the biggest fees for the investment bank and its brokerage unit."

"And," observed Sean, "the little guy who is at work only learns about the ratings change on the night's news, or in the newspaper the next day, or perhaps on Saturday evening, when he looks at his portfolio and sees a big gain or loss. By the time the little guy can act, much of the price move has already occurred."

"So, what do you conclude about investment analysts?" asked Sam.

Sean gave a succinct reply. "There are too many of them. Their primary role is to generate fees for their own investment bank. They do not add value for the individual investor."

He paused and continued, "There is no need for more than three analysts to follow any company. They usually come up with the same buy, sell, or hold recommendation. The rest are just an unnecessary cost for our economy. They can only be rationalized as an attempt by the investment banks to lure clients and get a piece of the fee pie for themselves."

After another pause, he concluded, "There are honest investment analysts who would like to serve the average investor. However, because of the nature of the business, the investor can't be sure who they are or what motivates the analyst on a particular recommendation. Even in the case of honest investment analysts, the big client gets the first call. It's sad, but the profession needs to shrink; it needs to focus on forecasts of financial statements, free cash flow growth rates, and Valuation Statements that provide real value to investors."[13]

"How does that help my friends?" asked Wendy.

"It provides a transparent estimate of the Enterprise Value of the company, that empowers the individual investor to determine if a stock is over-or undervalued at its current price," replied Sam.

"How so?" asked Wendy.

"Before we get to that, let's finish up with major distractions," replied Sam. "If we can learn to recognize them as distractions, I think that it will be easier for your friends to focus on the real value of a stock. Wendy, why don't you talk to us about the next distraction: investment bankers?"

Investment Bankers

"You are a hard man, McAllen," Wendy taunted. "OK, here goes. There are too many investment bankers, and they are overpaid relative to the value they add. They are some of the best snake-oil salesmen in the world, and the products they sell more often destroy rather than create value for Shareowners."

Sam and Sean laughed. They were surprised by Wendy's candor, especially considering that she was talking about her chosen profession. Wendy even laughed at herself.

After the laughter subsided, Sam wiped tears from his eyes and said, "I expected your comments to be honest, but more discrete. Before you describe why investment bankers are a distraction, tell us why you're still an investment banker."

"There is room for improvement, and more honest people, in every profession," she quipped. "Even investment banking."

"Touché," laughed Sam. "Continue."

"Maybe I should begin by discussing what investment bankers do," Wendy replied. "Basically, they are very sophisticated private brokers—they are salespeople. While regular brokers attempt to earn fees from the public or institutions, such as mutual funds, by providing market liquidity for standard securities like stocks and bonds, investment bankers do essentially the same thing for companies, governments, and very wealthy individuals, but with much greater sophistication."

"Explain that further," urged Sam.

Wendy obliged. "Investment bankers usually have direct access to senior corporate officers. As investment bankers approach a corporate CEO or CFO, they are basically approaching them with two agendas. 'Find a need and fill it' or 'Create a need and fill it.'"

"What's wrong with that?" inquired Sean.

"I'll let you be the judge," she replied. "Let me continue. The investment banker asks questions that elicit what the CEO and CFO are trying to achieve with the company. In the process, the investment banker learns how sophisticated the CEO and CFO are with respect to understanding whether it is GAAP accounting numbers, (for example earnings per share (EPS)) or growing the Enterprise Value (the net present value of cash flow) that creates value for a company. They also learn how the CEO and CFO's incentive plans are structured."

"Why does that matter?" asked Sean.

Wendy replied, "As you work with me and learn more about investment banking, you will discover a dirty secret to making money in investment banking. The secret is that many more products can be sold to a CEO who believes that growing accounting EPS creates value, than can be sold to a CEO who believes that value is created by increasing Enterprise Value (the net present value of cash flow). The problem for the Shareowner is that most investment banking products designed to create accounting EPS, such as off balance sheet financing, leveraged leasing, and mergers and acquisitions, actually cost the company more cash, and therefore destroy Enterprise Value."

She continued, "In addition, if a product enhances the CEO's and CFO's incentive payment, it is easier to sell a product to him, even if it doesn't create Enterprise Value for Shareowners. In other words, *CEOs and CFOs whose incentive plans are based on accounting earnings per share (EPS) will trade cash value for accounting numbers much more readily than CEOs who understand the concept of present value of cash flow and are paid to create Enterprise Value.*"

Sean seemed a little incredulous as he challenged her. "Give me an example."

"That's easy," Wendy responded. "I could give you many, but one is very obvious.

"CEOs do acquisitions for a variety of reasons, but often CEOs do them to 'grow' sales and EPS, which, coincidentally, increase their incentive payments. Well, the data is in and it is not convincing. A variety of universities, consulting firms, and business magazines have reviewed the results of acquirers versus their peers over different time periods, ranging from one to five years. As Sam said earlier, overall, the results indicate that in more than seventy percent of the cases, the acquirers underperformed their industry peers in sales growth, EPS growth, cash-flow growth, and share-price growth.[14] I am sure that if you look at the incentive plan payments, the CEOs got paid on the increased EPS that they bought in acquisitions, even though no Enterprise Value was added for Shareowners. *Regardless of the 'spin,' the bottom line is that CEOs paid away Shareowner cash value in order to generate accounting earnings on which their incentives were paid.*"

Sean shook his head in consternation and said, "Why would the investment bankers sell products that destroy a company's value? Why wouldn't they coach the CEOs on the right thing to do for Shareowners?"

Wendy replied promptly, "We could dance around all evening with apologetics for investment bankers. Some investment bankers try to do the right thing, but the bottom line is that senior investment bankers are personally paid multi-million-dollar incentives to generate fees for the investment banks, not to create Enterprise Value for the client's Shareowners. The investment bankers often earn more in bonuses than their client CEOs and CFOs. That's a strong incentive to close deals without regard for impact on the client."

Sam interjected, "Whoa. Let's step back and focus on who's really accountable here. Remember, Sean, it is the responsibility of the company's directors and Shareowners to motivate management to create Enterprise Value. If directors measure and pay management to do the wrong thing, it's not the responsibility of the investment bankers to train or re-motivate the CEOs. The only interest the investment bankers have in the company is to use it as a platform to generate fees for themselves."

Wendy continued, "There is another aspect to this, Sean. As we mentioned earlier, if several years later, a deal—for example, an acquisition—doesn't look good to the company, the investment banking community can earn another fee on the divestiture. Look at companies like Vivendi International and WorldCom, who were serial acquirers for years. In the end, due to heavy debt loads, they ended up selling off many of their acquisitions after destroying tens of billions of dollars in Shareowner value. The investment bankers earned tens of millions of dollars in fees once for the acquisitions and a second time for the divestitures. You can be sure that there is another investment banker on the other side of the deal earning fees by representing the buyer or seller's counterparty."

Sean shook his head in dismay. However, Sam brightened up and said, "Sean, as disenchanted as you may be, Wendy's comments contain the seeds of two ideas that we will use later to identify the cause and solution for the crisis in corporate responsibility."

"How so?" Sean asked.

Sam replied, "First, whether it is the CEO being paid on increasing accounting EPS, or the investment banker being paid on investment banking fees, their actions prove that *people do what you measure and pay them to do.*

"Second, as in the case of CEOs, *if you measure and pay people to do the wrong thing,* such as increasing accounting earnings per share rather than the increasing Enterprise Value (the present value of cash flow), *they will do the wrong thing. Actions follow measurement and pay. The challenge is to measure and pay people to do the right thing.*"

Recognition appeared on Sean's face as he nodded and said, "Really great insight, Sam."

But Wendy still looked troubled and shared another concern. "Sam, I think that investment bankers will always be a distraction for another reason."

Sam had a knowing frown on his face as he said, "Share it."

"Investment bankers are the most influential people in controlling the perception of value throughout the corporate securities chain," she replied. "Think about it. Whether you're talking about the issuer or the buyer of a company's security, the investment banker is influencing the perception of value, both from the buyer's and seller's points of view."

"Please elaborate," said Sean.

"Sure," she replied. "Through contacts with CEOs and CFOs, investment bankers influence what deals these people do, why they do them, and the price at which they do them. The deals either create or destroy Enterprise Value for the company, but they always generate fees for the investment banker. On the other hand, the investment bankers influence the investors' perception of value through the investment analysts, who hold sway on 'proper' levels of P/E ratios and growth rates used to identify the target price for a company's stock. The circle closes as the investment bankers use the investment analyst criteria to influence which deals are done by CEOs and CFOs, because 'It's what the investors want.'"

"Great insight, Wendy," said Sam. "A number of investment banking activities really do support the creation of Enterprise Value for Shareowners—for example, raising new money for a company's investment needs. But the more that you get into products involving acquisitions and accounting arbitrage to 'puff' EPS or to 'dress' balance sheets, the more that investment banking products destroy the cash value of the client company."

After a long pause in the conversation, Sam turned to Wendy. "Wendy, I get the impression from your earlier comments that you think politicians and regulators are distractions."

"Absolutely—who wouldn't?" replied Wendy.

Regulators

Wendy continued her observations on politicians and regulators. "I don't fault the politicians as distractions as much as I do the regulators. The regulators have a special public trust to live up to and the responsibility to act with the highest standards of professionalism. After all, they have a monopoly on the regulation of their industry. They are supposed to be experts and sensitive to the public's needs. If they make the wrong decisions, it hurts all of us, because imposing unnecessary regulations is like putting wrist and ankle weights on a marathon runner. They reduce a company's effectiveness in competing globally, and therefore reduce jobs or slow job growth."

"Explain further," Sam requested.

Wendy responded, "First, Sean and I have asked you to identify the unknown apparition that is haunting the markets causing the crisis in corporate responsibility. That should tell you that the regulators haven't convinced the markets that they have identified and addressed the 'root cause' of the crisis."

"You're right there," exclaimed Sean.

"Second," Wendy continued, "The regulators have failed us in obvious ways. Take Fed Chairman Alan Greenspan. When the stock markets were going to excessive price-to-earnings ratios in the 90s, he verbally wrung his hands by calling it 'irrational exuberance,' and then raised interest rates. If he had understood his business, he wouldn't have punished the real economy, Main Street, by raising interest rates and simultaneously raising unemployment. He would have increased margin requirements[15] on stock to address the inflation, a.k.a. speculation, in the equity markets. After all, the impact on equity markets of increasing margin requirements on equities is comparable to increasing interest rates to reduce inflation in the real economy. Furthermore, when speculation in equities continued after he had increased interest rates, rather than continuing his ineffective jawboning approach of blaming irrational exuberance, he should have increased margin requirements, or even considered that perhaps a structural problem existed requiring a completely different solution."

Wendy continued. "Harvey Pitt's failures as Chairman of the SEC are so notorious that I won't repeat them.[16] But, there is a generic point that I think my friends can take from his and Alan Greenspan's tenure. Regulators are always fighting the new war with the tools, strategies, and objectives of the last war. As a result, they fail to anticipate the next new problem and are too late to protect investors from it."

"Well said, Wendy," Sam observed. "I told the following story at the ranch last summer, but it bears repeating, because it dramatically illustrates the point that you are making.

"In the movie *Patton*, George C. Scott, who portrayed General Patton, was surveying a battlefield in which U.S. tanks had just beaten back a German advance in a costly battle. As I recall, the battle occurred near a line of concrete bunkers built by the French along their eastern border with Germany. The bunkers had heavy cannon that could only be pointed east in order to defend against a German invasion. The Germans had come around the north end of the line of bunkers and attacked from its rear. As he surveyed the fixed French fortifications known as the Maginot Line, Patton was quoted as saying:

Fixed fortifications are monuments to the stupidity of man. For if God's mountain ranges and oceans can be overcome, then anything built by man can be overcome."

Sam continued, "Like the Maginot Line, laws and regulations are static man-made defenses. As such, they are vulnerable in at least two ways. First, the rule writers can't anticipate every way that a motivated person can legally and in good conscience get around them. And, second, the rules are static in a dynamic world. Remember that we are dealing with very smart, highly-motivated people who are paid big incentives to increase earnings per share any way that they can. That's why you will hear me repeatedly say that *it is more effective to change peoples' goals rather than to erect fences to keep them away from their goals.*"

"Interesting," said Wendy. "In effect, by re-directing their energy and resources toward a new goal, people are regulating themselves away from doing things associated with the old goal."

"That's what effective free enterprise is supposed to do," observed Sam.

After a pause, Sam said, "Are there other distractions that we ought to make your friends aware of?"

"Yes," replied Sean. "Pop finance."

Financial Media

"Pop finance?" said Wendy in a surprised voice. "What is pop finance?"

"Pop finance is like pop music and 'pop-perp law enforcement,'" said Sean. "It's the fad of the moment. Once the fad wears off, it's on to something new. Pop finance is financial stories that titillate people in much the way that stories are chosen for the entertainment page. They are chosen to sell airtime or ads rather than to solve a problem or provide genuine analysis."

"Why is that a distraction?" asked Wendy.

Sean replied, "If a finance show or financial column is really entertainment disguised as information, then it's a big distraction for your friends. It diverts their attention from what really matters."

"Let's put this in a different context," Sam suggested. "*Follow the money.* How do people in the financial media get paid?"

Sean responded, "By filling air or print space with stories that attract readers and sell ads."

"And what happens when media space expands with the proliferation of new financial cable channels, newspapers, and magazines?" inquired Sam.

"Media inflation," responded Wendy. "They have to fill air-time quickly with opinions that they think will attract readership or viewers."

Sam asked, "Do you suppose that media inflation leads to higher-quality information, or merely entertainment, in the form of financial 'reality' shows that are anything but reality?"

Sam didn't expect an answer; they smiled as he moved on. "Perhaps there are some questions that your friends should ask themselves when trying to determine if a particular element of the financial media is a distraction. They should be asking, 'What experience does the reporter have that qualifies him to select and slant the financial information in the stories? Has the reporter ever had to personally create value in a company, or has he ever managed a portfolio? If so, what was his track record?'"

Sam continued, "A second set of questions is equally to the point. 'Who is monitoring the reporter's ethical standards?' After all, wasn't it the talk-show media that took payments from drug companies to plug legitimate drugs as part of their shows? In other words, the media presented paid-programming as if it were independent journalism.

"Another thought for your friends: While the media will ask financial analysts if they or their firm own the stock being touted, who asks the reporter if the reporter owns the stock? After all, the reporter, or the producer, selects the analysts and often the stocks that are discussed on the show."

After a pause, Sean shook his head and said, "No one—and certainly not the financial media—has a 'get out of jail free' card when it comes to distractions. For all these reasons and more, the media is still clueless as to the real cause of this crisis in corporate responsibility. They are still writing stories about greedy executives rather than digging to get to the root of the crisis. If it weren't for the 'perp walk' photo ops, the financial reporters would merely be reading more stock prices or analyst reports on the air. Perhaps the networks could save money by using computer-generated digital celebrities to read the reports."

Sam chuckled, then commented, "If no one has a 'get out of jail free' card, then I suppose I can suggest that accountants, and even accounting itself, is a distraction."

"I feel a point coming," said Sean as he winked at Wendy.

Wendy laughed and joined the game by suggesting, "Sam, why don't *you* explain why you think accountants and accounting are distractions and give us a chance to eat?"

"Fair enough," said Sam. "Let me talk about accounting before turning to the accounting industry."

Accounting

"Accounting is a distraction for most people because they think of it in the same way that they think about science or mathematics," said Sam.

"Come again?" said Wendy.

Sam replied, "Most people consider science or mathematics to be derived from natural laws or rules of logic that are inviolate. For the average person, generally accepted accounting principles have historically held a similar mystique. The implication for the average layman is that there is only one right way to measure income, and that is the way prescribed by GAAP accounting standards."

"Wrong," laughed Sean in agreement. "*Accounting is nothing more than a mathematical model of a business.*"

"Right," Sam agreed. "And like all other mathematical models, accounting is an imperfect approximation of part of the real world. While some math models are better than others, almost all of them need to evolve and be revised as our understanding of the universe advances."

Sam continued, "For example, Sir Isaac Newton developed his Laws of Motion in the seventeenth century to describe how gravity and other forces cause a body to move. Engineers still use Newton's Laws today for engineering work in everyday life. But, three centuries later, Einstein recognized that Newton's Laws did not accurately describe motion at the high speeds in space or provide an adequate basis for studying the building blocks of the universe, such as electrons, protons, and neutrons. So he devised a new mathematical model, $E = mc^2$, and the Theory of Relativity, which displaced Newton's Laws of Motion in high-speed environments. Without Einstein's new model, we could not travel in space, benefit from medical tools like x-rays, or enjoy many of life's luxuries, such as satellite TV."

"So, what is the problem?" asked Wendy.

"There are two problems," Sam replied. "The first is the public's belief that accounting has the stature of a natural or mathematical 'law,' which can't be challenged. The second problem is that the accounting model has not changed and evolved with the world around it."

"Wait, Sam, that isn't true," said Wendy. "There are over 150 different Financial Accounting Standards (FAS) that are constantly evolving—not to mention their predecessors, such as the Accounting Principles Board Opinions and Accounting Research Bulletins, which are in effect until superseded."

"Ahhh, there's where accounting's second deception caught you," replied Sam.

"What do you mean?" challenged Wendy.

Sam replied, "*All these changes to the GAAP standards merely tweak the means of measuring components of the GAAP financials. They haven't changed the fundamental measurement objective of the GAAP accounting model. That objective remains the same, as it has over the past 200 years.* The accounting model is still based on the premise that spreading historic costs against revenue is an accurate way to measure the value of a company. It presumes that whatever is left over after recovering historic costs increases or decreases the Shareowner's value in the company. They even misuse Shareowners' Value to mean Shareowners' book equity."

Sam continued, "The whole concept of the mathematical model which we call accounting was built in a slower-moving world for the benefit of creditors. It was designed to tell lenders if there was enough collateral in the company and if there was enough safety cushion—called shareholder's equity—to protect their loans. This 'historic-cost' model was a good approximation for both lenders and Shareowners in a slow-moving world where there were very few liquid markets for Shareowners' stock, and where it took decades for products and technology to become obsolete."

Sam became animated. "But in a fast-moving world with liquid equity markets, and a world in which technology, products, and markets are often made obsolete in two years, it makes no sense to use the historic-cost model to measure the value of a firm. In fact, with the creation of Financial Accounting Standard 142 on *Goodwill and Other Intangible Assets,* the accountants themselves explicitly recognized that using historic costs to value an acquisition—i.e., a company within a company—was no longer relevant. Newer math models, such as those which calculate the present value of cash flow, are required to annually determine the Enterprise Value of the acquired companies."

"You are right," said Sean. "We have just seen a capital mania flood the telecom industry with too much 'free' equity capital, and within four years it turned a new, capital-intensive, value-added business into a commodity market with extreme overcapacity. Tens of billions of dollars of Shareowner equity will have to be written off the accounting books at companies like Quest Communications and WorldCom, but it is happening at least two years after the problem was recognized by the decline in the telecom stocks' market price."

"Sam, you have said a lot here," said Wendy, "but this seems pretty complicated and could take a long time to figure out."

"No," said Sam. "There are two easy, elegant solutions. Individuals can use one solution in their personal investing until the accounting industry adopts the second as a national solution, voluntarily or otherwise. Both solutions involve one simple key change to the accounting model."

Sam paused and Wendy immediately spoke up. "What change?"

Sam replied, "To charge the company a return on the market value of the equity it uses, and to present it in the form of a Valuation Statement."

"So," said Wendy, "in explaining accounting as a distraction to my friends, I point out that accounting is a mathematical model designed for a slower-moving world. It is still predicated on the same concepts of spreading historic costs that it used 200 years ago. I should challenge my friends to name any other discipline that hasn't changed in over 200 years. Why, even our concept of the Laws of Motion have changed with the introduction of Einstein's Theory of Relativity."

"You can also explain it another way," offered Sean.

"How's that?" asked Wendy.

"You can point out to your friends that using historic costs without a charge for the use of Shareowners' capital is like driving the hairpin turns of a Grand Prix race by looking in the rear view mirror."

"Very graphic," Sam said, smiling, "but it's true. You can't visualize, let alone create, the future by living in the past."

"Why haven't the accountants done anything about the GAAP model?" asked Wendy with a touch of agitation in her voice.

"Good question," said Sam. "Let's talk about the accountants."

Accountants

Sam took a long drink of iced tea. His face showed reluctance yet conviction as he began. "There are many hard-working, honest, dedicated people in the accounting industry. But their sincerity doesn't alter the industry's collective failure in serving both the Shareowner and society's changed needs."

Sam slowly looked each of them in the eyes as he said, "One of the great distractions is the public perception that accounting is a profession. It could be, but it isn't."

He continued, "The reality is that the CPA certificate is a membership card in a white collar union, not the symbol of membership in a profession."

"Wow," said Sean. "If any accountants heard you say that, they would be pretty upset."

"Only if they failed to be honest with themselves about the results of their collective actions," replied Sam. "It's within their power to change, but they haven't."

Sam shifted in his chair and continued, "The public perception of accounting as a profession lulls the public into a false sense of security by giving accounting an air of credibility that is both misplaced and unwarranted. The truth is that *the way accounting is currently practiced, accounting is nothing more than another industry.*"

"Sam, before you explain that statement, please go back," said Wendy. "What's the difference between a profession and an industry?"

"Good question. The difference is very clear, as are the practical consequences," replied Sam.

Sam drank some more iced tea. "A profession is a group of people, trained and practicing a particular discipline, who also feel a higher calling both to a code of ethics in practicing the discipline and a higher calling to advancing the knowledge and practice of the profession in serving mankind. Examples of professions include doctors and engineers."

Sam continued. "An industry, on the other hand, is merely a group of people who earn a living producing or providing a similar product or service. They may have an industry group to lobby government lawmakers and regulators—to set industry standards such as GAAP accounting and auditing standards and to limit membership in order to keep income up or to provide member training—but, they do not motivate the individual members by identifying a mission of higher service to mankind through the advancement of the core knowledge and practice of the whole industry."

"Sam," said Wendy. "I still don't see how the accounting industry is a distraction."

"Simple," said Sam. "The fact that the accounting industry positions itself as a profession instead of a trade group lulls all of us into the false sense of security. We assume that accountants are a group of professionals committed to better measurement of business in order to serve Shareowners and other business constituents. By assuming that this is true, our society has failed to investigate whether they are indeed performing these functions at a level that we should expect of professionals."

"What did we miss?" asked Wendy.

"Let me name a few things," replied Sam. "First, by assuming that accountants were professionals committed to a higher purpose, Arthur Andersen was allowed to get off with wrist slaps on failed audits like Sunbeam, Waste Management, and others that occurred many years before problems surfaced in its audits of Enron and WorldCom.[17] It was assumed that Andersen had made honest mistakes and that, as professionals, they wanted to proactively prevent recurrences of the same audit failures. Unfortunately, the public and regulators did not perceive that Andersen's profit culture was overwhelming the firm's 'professional' standards.[18] Another example: look at the way that the accounting industry has waffled for years on requiring that the cost of employee stock options be included as an expense on the income statement. Employee stock options are clearly quantifiable costs of doing business, just like pension and healthcare expenses. They become liabilities that should be expensed beginning on the date that they are granted to employees."

Sean asked, "Why don't the accountants require option costs to be shown as an expense?"

Sam responded, "Because, although option accounting is in transition, reporting option expense on the income statement is 'optional' under GAAP. As such, any accountant who requires option expensing puts his auditing fees in jeopardy by coming into conflict with their client's CEOs in at least two ways. First, it more clearly reveals how much the CEO is being paid. Second, the expense reduces earnings per share, on which the client CEO earns his bonus. Companies in Silicon Valley and dot-coms complained to politicians in Washington that showing the option expense on the income statements hurts innovation. The fact is that in many cases, these companies do not have a business model or a product that justifies their company unless they hide compensation costs, which reduce the Enterprise Value for Shareowners."

Sam looked at Wendy. "If you want more examples of why accounting is an industry rather than a profession, I suggest that you read a history or two of the evolution of accounting in the U.S.[19] It is the history of an industry filled with industry politics and only briefly interspersed with flickers of professionalism—not the other way around."

Sam shook his head and continued, "Professionals make mistakes, but they are honest mistakes; they learn from them, and they try not to repeat them. Let me give an example using the engineering profession. Remember the famous film of the Tacoma Narrows Bridge in Tacoma, Washington? When opened in the middle of 1940, its 5,000-foot length made it the third-longest suspension bridge in the world. Only months after its completion, wind induced oscillations caused the bridge to go into twenty-eight-foot-high undulations and a two-wave twisting motion that tilted the roadbed forty-five degrees in either direction. At 11:00 a.m. on November 7, 1940, the bridge roadbed collapsed and fell over 190 feet into Puget Sound. The bridge was rebuilt four years later, but only after engineers had developed a whole new set of math theories on aerodynamics, vibration, harmonics, and wave phenomenon, and had tested them in a wind tunnel. Every major suspension bridge worldwide in existence at the time was checked in light of the new models. And ever since then, these new math models have been used in the design of major suspension-bridge structures."

Sam concluded, "Imagine if the engineering or medical professions had made no fundamental advances in knowledge or practice in the last 200 years. No one would fly, we would all be riding horses, there would be no electricity or telephone, the medical profession would still be bleeding people to cure illnesses, and we would all have wooden false teeth like some people in George Washington's times."

"But wait," said Wendy. "Accountants have adopted new technology and are using computers to manage data faster and better. And they now use variations, such as cost and inflation accounting."

"You are proving my point," said Sam. "As an industry, accountants are using technology developed by other industries to earn consulting fees; they are merely doing their existing measurement jobs cheaper and faster to increase profits. However, *they are only improving the GAAP model after it cracks or fails, rather than in anticipation of a measurement problem or need.* For example, inflation accounting was only introduced after years of high inflation in the U.S. and overseas in the 1970s. As a group, accountants are not systematically challenging the alignment of the GAAP model with what society needs it to measure. They have not defined a mission statement that will produce the next quantum leap which will serve mankind better, such as relativity or applied aerodynamics."

"Sam, what would you have them do?" asked Wendy.

Sam replied, "I would have them think about their real role and then define a mission statement for the profession that is consistent with society's need for them."

Sean asked, "For example?"

Sam thought for a moment and said, "Society needs a profession that can measure whether businesses are allocating capital effectively, i.e., creating economic value by earning more than the cost of capital being used. That's the real source of new products and higher living standards for all of us. So, if there really were an accounting profession, the mission statement should be aligned with this objective. I think that a mission statement for the accounting profession would include ethics statements similar to those in other professions, but it would also have a vision statement that included the following:

Our role is to measure and to make continuous improvements in—

1. The contemporaneous measurement of the economic value of the firm at a *point in time*

2. The measurement of the contemporaneous economic value created by the firm *over time*."

Sam elaborated, "Accountants have been given a special trust by our society. *Measurement is at the heart of how we interpret results and motivate people.* When accountants say something, which either presents or interprets business numbers, it is believed as an undeniable truth. As a consequence, *accountants have a responsibility not only to measure accurately but also to measure the right things.* Remember a lesson from the quality process. If you measure and correct the wrong thing, you still produce defects. As a society, we are producing defective companies, companies that destroy economic value (Enterprise Value) by failing to allocate capital effectively and by not earning the cost of capital that they are using. This is happening because we are measuring the wrong things."

He continued, "It is still important to provide information for asset-based creditors. However, accountants must collectively have the intellectual integrity to admit that GAAP no longer addresses society's primary measurement need: to measure the creation of economic value (Enterprise Value). Times have changed, and accountants must refocus their mission and GAAP to measure economic value."

Sam paused and then added, "I am very concerned about whether accountants will recognize the need to change, or whether public reaction and increased regulation is going to cause them to regress. If, in self-defense, they regress into a body of rule-enforcers, it may lead to a tyranny of the accountants and the continued destruction of economic value for society—all of this as a result of using a misdirected measurement system."

Wendy asked, "Can you explain that?"

Sam nodded. "Recently, a 15-year veteran CFO of a 3.5-million NYSE company was fired by the CEO. The reason was unusual. This fifteen-year veteran CFO was not a CPA, but had asked the auditing firm to provide a certificate about the scope of their ongoing audit. They refused and asked for the CFO to be fired. According to the accounting firm, there were no disputes with the firm's financials.[20]

"No CFO—even if he is a CPA—is going to understand all of the technical details of accounting. As a result, he has to rely on the auditors for special accounting and tax expertise. In addition, in the wake of failed audits by Andersen and other major accounting firms, it is completely reasonable for a CFO to demand that auditors stand accountable for the content and scope of their work. It is not in society's best interest to create an environment in which an auditor can threaten not to certify a firm's financials unless the audit firm gets its own way without a logical reason. Instead of a check and balance, auditors' actions will become a tyranny as they attempt to reduce their own liability for audits. We will see more of this behavior from the very industry that has already failed society by failing to measure the creation of economic value."

Sam concluded, "I'll share more insights on this when we talk about the true cause of the crisis in corporate responsibility. Let's move on to some more tangible distractions."

Everyone at the table sat in subdued silence after this exposition. They saw that, collectively, the 340,000 CPAs had let the country down in a *material* way. Wendy and Sean knew that the accountants would not correct the problem by themselves. Their vested interest in the status quo, in fees and in reducing their own legal liability, was too great.

After a few moments, Sean said, "How about discussing executive compensation as a distraction?"

Executive Compensation

Sam smiled and said, "Executive compensation is a titillating distraction. But it is not worth spending a lot of time on here, except to say that the fundamental cause of excessive compensation is the failure of our measurement system to include the cost of equity as a cost of doing business."

"That's a new one," said Wendy. "I thought that you were going to blame poor plan design by human resources or boards of directors who were asleep at the switch."

Sam smiled, but remained focused on the issue. "The culprit is the illusion that companies are making money when they really aren't."

"What do you mean?" asked Wendy.

Sam turned to Wendy. "If a CEO is losing money for you, you pay him differently than if he is making money for you."

Wendy repeated, "As I said…what do you mean?"

Sam smiled and replied, "Suppose a big company that wasn't growing cash flow had a market value of $50 billion and had net income of $2 billion. Let's further assume that the $2-billion net income had just increased 33 percent, or

$500 million, over the prior year. The board of directors might say, 'Why that's great, let's pay the CEO a $20-million bonus.'"

Sam continued, "But that $50 billion of equity has a cost—it's the return that needs to be earned for the Shareowner to justify his owning the stock. As we will discuss later, the Shareowner should expect at least a ten percent after-tax return. That's a $5-billion required return on the Shareowners' $50-billion investment ($50 billion x 10%). The company only earned $2 billion before the cost of equity. After subtracting the $5 billion 'cost of equity,' the company lost $3 billion for its Shareowners. How is this CEO entitled to any incentive when he is losing money for the Shareowners?"

"How much should a CEO be paid?" Wendy challenged.

Sam replied, "Any CEO who is paid more than $5 million a year, including incentives, is in the entertainment business."

Wendy and Sean sat silently as they considered Sam's insights.

Finally, Sean quietly observed, "You're right. It's pretty hard to lead when your followers are focused on your pay and perks rather than on where you are trying to lead them."

Sam added, "In general, CEOs are smart, hard-working people. However, *uniqueness of a position does not make the occupant unique.* Simply because someone is the CEO when an inevitable decision has to be made doesn't mean that he should get the spoils of that decision. In free enterprise, the spoils belong to the person who risked the capital. The CEO's role is to lead the employees in growing the Enterprise Value (the present value of cash flow) of the company. Teams win games, not quarterbacks. What happens to a company's cohesiveness when a CEO gets a $25-million payday that's earned on the backs of employees through job cuts and cuts in retirement and medical benefits? That CEO isn't going to have the credibility to lead. He can only administer further cuts. Administrators can't inspire growth. Cost-cutting isn't the type of insight that should be rewarded with $2-million paydays. Continuous cost-cutting is a requirement for survival these days, as is continuous improvement of the company's product or service.

"The CEO job is not a lottery ticket. It is a call to leadership and warrants compensation commensurate to the Enterprise Value he or she creates for the company.

"We all need to remember something. *A company's profits are meant to reward the Shareowners for the risk that they take in letting employees, including the CEO, use their Shareowner's capital in order to earn a living and a fair wage.* Five-million-dollar-plus paydays, even if they are stock options, are excessive, come right out of the Shareowner's pocket, and distract from the creation of Enterprise Value."

Sam concluded, "When someone like Bill Gates of Microsoft earns several hundred million dollars in dividends, that's great. He is earning the dividends based on the capital he invested in the business. It's his Shareowner return for risking his capital. Those dividends are separate from his compensation, including stock options, as Microsoft's CEO, which properly reflects his contributions in creating Enterprise Value for Shareowners."

After a long pause, Sean suggested, "Let's discuss directors as a distraction."

"Let's," Wendy seconded.

Directors

Sean volunteered, "Until Enron, the average Shareowner had become complacent. They thought that prestigious board members were ensuring that management was acting responsibly in the Shareowner's interests. But with the advent of Enron's public problems, people began to realize that their faith in directors had been misplaced."

"I think you're right," said Wendy. "Failures in corporate governance at other companies became obvious, for example, $50-million-plus paydays for CEOs at otherwise reputable companies when no Enterprise Value was being created. Furthermore, excessive retirement perks for many, including Jack Welch at GE, unjustified multimillion-dollar loans to executives, such as at Tyco, and failures of acquisitions to add value because of excessive purchase prices have all made Shareowners question directors' motivations and capabilities."

Sam said, "You are right, Wendy. Shareowners are questioning not only that, but also whether directors have learned from past mistakes at other companies. You know this is not the first time in recent memory that director reforms were attempted. In the early 1990s, directors had to change their CEOs at IBM, GM, American Express, Kodak, Westinghouse, and Apple Computer, among others.[21] In retrospect, the performance of some of those CEOs wasn't as bad as what we're seeing today. But directors did not collectively learn from those experiences of the early 1990s, and none of the reforms in the 90s created a collective memory among directors to prevent recurrence of the same mistakes."

Sam added, "*The problem with director performance is twofold. First*, based on directors that I have met, *less than two in ten really understand that management creates value in a company by increasing Enterprise Value* and not by arbitraging accounting rules to increase earnings per share. *Second, directors don't have the collective memory or continuity of focus that only comes from measuring the right thing.*

This is a problem principally because they use the same GAAP accounting measures as management. They are not measuring management's performance based on increasing Enterprise Value."

"How do we fix it?" asked Sean.

"Well," Sam replied, "I don't have a lot of faith in 'soft' solutions, such as electing 'outside' directors or hiring 'corporate governance' officers. Outside directors are humans and are subject to the same influences as any other human, including the charm of a charismatic CEO. Corporate governance officers are the sign of a weak board as well as the sign of a company that is more interested in avoiding regulatory action or a lawsuit by box-checking rather than being proactive in trying to create value."

Sam concluded, "*Because circumstances are always changing, the only real protection that a Shareowner has on the board is in the hands of individual directors with backbone who understand both their fiduciary duties to Shareowners and how value is created for Shareowners.* You don't get that from checking boxes; new circumstances aren't on a checklist. I believe that all the virtues of good directorship spring from holding the directors and management accountable to a measure that creates Enterprise Value for Shareowners. *Use of measurement provides focus and continuity over time.* What gets measured gets done. It is also surprising how accountability to the right measure strengthens people's backbone in other critical virtues."

Wendy observed, "What you are really saying, Sam, is something that I haven't heard anyone address. You're saying that the real failure in corporate governance is at the national level. It is the failure to measure and pay for the right thing, the creation of Enterprise Value."

Sam looked her in the eyes and said, "Right on." It was clear that he was losing taste for the subject and was ready to move on, so he said, "Let's order dessert."

5

The Grand Deception

Sean ordered a *Choco-l'Eight*, and Wendy and Sam ordered coffee. While waiting for desert, Sam mentioned that he was planning to meet Georgia and Tom Roman for breakfast. Wendy and Sean remembered the husband-and-wife long-distance trucking team from the ST Bar ranch that past summer. Sam mentioned that Georgia had called him a number of times recently to explore investment ideas, and he suggested that Wendy and Sean join him for breakfast so that they could discuss a shorthand technique for benchmarking the value of a stock. Wendy and Sean said that it would be fun to see the Romans again and that they would be pleased to join him for breakfast.

When dessert and coffee arrived, Sean immediately commenced devouring an oversized Choco-l'Eight sufficient for three people. The sweet consisted of moist chocolate cake with chocolate icing covered by chocolate and chocolate-chip ice cream, smothered under hot fudge, and topped with chocolate whipped cream, a chocolate wafer-cookie, and sprinkles of chocolate candy.

Sam turned to Wendy. "Ah, the naive excesses and indulgences of youth."

"Reminds you of a Greater Fool," Wendy said, laughing.

Sean kept his cool and merely exaggerated his movements as he brandished a loaded fork at them and sensuously devoured another piece of Choco-l'Eight.

They sat quietly drinking coffee, watching Sean and enjoying each other's company. From the corner of her eye, Wendy studied Sam. Her experience observing body language as an investment banker told her that Sam had been holding back something important.

She waited for the right moment and then said, "Sam, there's something important on your mind that you haven't shared with us. What is it?"

Sam looked at her, smiled, and replied. "You know your business well, young lady."

He paused, continued smiling, as he looked into his coffee, and spoke again. "Let me share with you what I believe is the greatest distraction. It is the one which is at the heart of this crisis in corporate responsibility."

With that, even Sean stopped eating. They both focused on Sam.

Sam continued, "I believe that the greatest distraction is really a deception."

Wendy whispered, "A deception?"

Sam replied, "It is the deception perpetrated by generations of accountants with a failed accounting vision and a deficient mathematical model, called GAAP accounting." He paused.

Finally, the suspense overcame Sean; he asked, "What is it?"

Sam replied, "It's the deception that equity is free."

He paused again while the idea percolated. Finally he urged, "Think about it. As I hinted at a moment ago, the income statement reports sales revenues and then subtracts the cost of the resources to produce those sales. For example, it subtracts the cost of raw material, the cost of labor, and the cost of buildings, sales commissions, executive bonuses, and interest expense on borrowed money. Why, it even subtracts the cost of government in the form of taxes. What is left is supposed to be for the Shareowner. In essence, the return to the Shareowner for the use of his capital is an afterthought—the leftovers."

Sam showed them a napkin sketch as he said, "Here is what 'Leftover Accounting' looks like."

Leftover Accounting

Sales:		$1,000
Less:	Costs of Materials, Labor, Equipment, Buildings, Selling & Administrative Expense, Management Pay	
	Subtotal:	(700)
	Interest	(150)
	Taxes	(50)
Left Over for Shareowners:	Net Income	$100 *

* If the company had 10 shares outstanding,
the earnings per share (EPS) would be $100/10 shares = $10 per share.

Sam became more animated as he said, "*But it doesn't make sense to simply say that whatever is leftover is sufficient to pay for the Shareowner's investment.* Common sense tells the average Shareowner that he has to earn a return on his investment. And simple logic tells him that his return is a cost to the company. This common sense is supported by more than fifty years of academic research and market practice, which have demonstrated that equity isn't free. Equity has a very well-determined cost. *The Shareowner's cost to invest in a company is at least equal to what the Shareowner could have earned by investing in the stock market as a whole.* For example, the cost is equal to what the Shareowner could have earned over the long run by investing in the Standard and Poors 500 stock index."

"I see where you're going," said Sean. "You're saying that when something is not shown as an expense in the income statement, people treat it as being free. So in this case, directors, CEOs, managers, employees, and the general public think that Shareowners' equity is free."

"Right on," said Sam. "And what happens when something is free?"

"Well, if I put it in the same context as time, water, and air, it is usually abused," observed Wendy.

"Absolutely right," said Sam.

"*As long as society permits accountants and the financial statements they create to perpetuate the myth that equity is free, society will be deceived into thinking that companies are creating economic value, when in fact, CEOs are being paid incentives to destroy it,*" said Sam.

"So let me see if I understand," said Wendy. "You are saying that we need to develop a 'Shareowners' P&L' by adding another expense line to the income statement in order to show a cost for the market value of the equity that Shareowners are investing in the company."

Wendy modified Sam's sketch by adding the cost of Shareowners' equity, as she said, "For example, if this company had no growth and its market value was $1.5 billion, then Shareowners should expect to earn 10 percent, or $150 million, just to keep the stock price where it is. When the $150-million cost of Shareowner capital is subtracted from the income statement, we find that the company didn't make $100 million, it actually lost $50 million for Shareowners. That's a loss of $5 per share instead of a profit of $10 per share on the 10 million shares."

Shareowners' Profit & Loss
(All numbers in millions)

Sales: $1,000

Less: Costs of Materials, Labor,
       Equipment, Buildings,
       Selling & Administrative
       Expense, Management Pay

                              Subtotal: (700)

                    Interest   (150)
                    Taxes   (50)

~~Left Over for Shareowners:~~ ~~Net Income~~   ~~$100~~

Cost of   (10 shares x $150 =
Shareowner's $1,500 Market Value)
Equity $1,500 x 10%* = $150   (150)

                    Shareowners'   ($50)**
                    Profit (Loss)

* Two percent inflation plus eight percent.
** The earnings per share is ($50)/10 shares = ($5)

Sean volunteered, "If Shareowners and directors looked at it that way, it would sure change the way that companies were managed as well as what CEOs were paid.

"That's right," said Sam. "*When a company is losing money instead of making it, it is managed differently, people are paid differently, and Shareowners make investment decisions differently.*"

Sam then turned to Wendy. "Wendy, your suggestion for modifying the income statement would be one way to start. But you are still starting with an income statement that is based on spreading historic costs. The real solution is to add a fourth GAAP financial statement, a Valuation Statement.[1] This statement will provide the Shareowner with an accurate calculation of the company's no-growth Enterprise Value, together with examples of what the Enterprise Value would be at different growth rates. The Shareowner can then select a growth rate and compare that Enterprise Value to the stock's current market price in order to decide whether to buy, sell, hold, or ignore the stock."

"Why haven't the accountants already created a Valuation Statement?" asked Wendy.

Sean replied, "As Sam said, accountants are part of a white-collar union interested in protecting their fees by not rocking the boat. They do not want to do anything that comes into conflict with the CEOs who are paying their fees. Changing the financial statements would show that most U.S. companies are not currently earning their cost of capital and must depend on growth to make up the shortfall. The question is whether these companies have the right amount of the right type of growth to make up the deficit. When these issues are clearly in focus, directors and Shareowners will realize that $5-million-plus annual paydays for CEOs cannot be justified. The excessive CEO paydays have no relationship to economic value being created by management for the Shareowner."

Sam nodded agreement. "*Fundamentally, accountants lack the vision of their role in society. They do not understand that through their measurements, they are the architects of our business culture and determine how society creates economic value—in other words, what gets measured gets done. How well they do their job determines our standard of living and our children's economic freedom.*"

Wendy urged Sam to continue, but Sam turned to her and said, "Not tonight. It's 10:30, and Sean looks tired after all the energy he expended eating his Choco-l'Eight."

---

1.   The Appendix contains a proposed Valuation Statement.

The trio laughed, finished coffee over small talk and then departed for their hotels.

Before Wendy fell asleep, she reflected on the evening's conversation. She liked what she'd heard and knew that it would help her friends to avoid distractions. She could hardly wait until breakfast to learn how Sam could convert these ideas into a simple method that her friends could use to benchmark stock values. And she could hardly wait to learn Sam's solution to the crisis in corporate responsibility.

PART III
Money Ain't Free

6

Cracker Barrel

It was a typically crisp December morning in Naperville, Illinois. Cars flew by on I-88, carrying their commuting passengers thirty miles east to Chicago. As Sam walked across the Cracker Barrel's parking lot, he reveled in the beauty of an explosive coral sunrise in the eastern sky. The wind, biting into his cheeks with its minus-15-degree wind chill, made Sam feel like he was back in the Rockies. By the time he walked through the second set of doors he had left the raw wind behind and his senses were awakening to the cheery atmosphere and the visual treat of the Cracker Barrel's general store, decorated with its Christmas lights and gifts. But Sam's favorite morning senses were reawakened when the hostess seated him at the table in front of the giant stone fireplace, with its crackling wood fire. The inviting, biting aroma of the hickory wood, the pungent odor of coffee, and the tantalizingly sweet smell of maple syrup reminded him of why Cracker Barrel was his breakfast haunt away from the ST Bar ranch.

The clock showed 6:05. He had arrived early intentionally. The morning's tranquility yielded to meditation. He ordered a cup of coffee and sipped it at the oak table while he watched the fire and thought over the prior evening's conversation. He understood why Wendy's friends, and so many others, were confused by the distractions they had discussed. He just wished that he could give them the confidence that they all deserved to invest in stocks. He had a big responsibility to Wendy this morning.

As he savored his coffee, enjoying the early-morning silence and lost in thought, he became conscious of two strong, gentle hands kneading his shoulder and neck muscles in a sensual, comforting rhythm. He sat absorbing it, unconcerned about the source of this warm, comforting gesture. Knowing that this soothing massage would end when he turned around, he held out as long as he dared, and then he reluctantly looked up to see a generous, playful grin on Georgia Roman's handsome face. Before he could get up, his neck was engulfed from behind with a bear hug, almost strangling him in the process, and Georgia plopped down in the chair beside him.

"All we need is some really strong ST Bar coffee and some humming birds, and we would be back on the lodge porch," she said.

"It might be a bit cold there, right now," he said. "Gosh, it's good to see you again Georgia. Where did you leave Tom?"

"Tom had to take the rig over to pick up an early load, and I asked him to drop me off early so that I could do a little shopping for our grandkids before I joined you for breakfast. Tom and I are going to spend Christmas with them in Minnesota in a few weeks. While I was looking around at the toys, I happened to see this old cowboy sitting over by the fire, and I thought I'd see if I could strike up a little romance."

Sam gave another one of his big grins and hearty laughs and said, "Absolutely," as he squeezed her hand. "Say, I'm glad that you are going to have breakfast with me. You remember Wendy and Sean from the ranch last summer?"

"Sure," replied Georgia.

"Well," Sam continued, "they will be getting here about 7:00, and we'll be continuing a conversation that we started last evening about how to help her friends regain confidence in stock investing."

"Sounds a little like what we were talking about at the ranch last summer. Fill me in," she said. "I'd like to join the conversation when they arrive."

After ordering coffee for Georgia and a refill for himself, Sam explained Wendy's concern for her friends and her need to give them a simpler way to benchmark the value of a stock. Sam then enjoyed Georgia's stories about adventures that she and her husband, Tom, were having in the 18-wheeler as the long-distance trucking team crisscrossed the country.

Wendy and Sean arrived a few minutes before seven. Wendy was bright-eyed and ready to go. Sean was dragging. Sam ribbed him about going soft ever since he 'went east.' Sean responded that young people needed their sleep.

Sam laughed at being bested by the implication.

After they exchanged greetings and ordered breakfast, Wendy got right to the point as she said, "OK, Sam, we have discussed the distractions, now let's get to the main show. How can my friends benchmark a stock to see if it is over-or undervalued?"

"That's what we're here for," replied Sam as he turned to Georgia. "As I mentioned last evening, Georgia and I have been discussing this very subject for several months, and I think that your friends would benefit from her insights. In fact, not only will it help your friends in their personal investing, but I think it will help them to understand the real cause and solution to this corporate crisis."

7

First Things First

As Georgia picked up the conversation with enthusiasm, Wendy recalled the extremely perceptive no-nonsense observations that Georgia had made at the ranch that past summer when they discussed how *both* Shareowners and managers create value for Shareowners.

"Well, as you know, I trade our personal retirement accounts using a wireless computer while our rig is rolling," Georgia began. "Tom and I make our own investment decisions, because we agreed that other people don't have the same interest in our financial success that we do. Their interest in our money is to earn fees for themselves—sweet and simple. If they lose some of our money, they don't have to live on a lower income. They can simply walk away. We can't."

Then, turning toward Wendy, Georgia cut to the chase. "Wendy, you need to tell your friends that *the most important thing that an investor must know is his goal.* Knowing your goal keeps you focused. Without that, every current fad and every news story will distract you."

Georgia paused to let Wendy absorb her point.

Finally, Wendy asked the obvious question, "Georgia, what's your goal?"

Georgia responded without hesitation, *"As a Shareowner, my goal is to have more cash in my pocket at the end of each day."* She added, *"As a Shareowner, I only get paid if I take actions that produce a cash return on my cash investment.* I don't get paid because I own certain industries, like tech or pharmaceuticals or financials. And I don't get paid because I own certain stocks, like IBM or Abbott, Baxter Labs or Citigroup. I don't get paid because accounting earnings go up. I only get paid if the cash value of my stock goes up."

Sam interjected, "Now, obviously, Georgia, you are *not* saying your stock investments have to grow and create cash each and every day or you will sell them."

"Right," said Georgia. "I am just pointing out that over any investment period, my stocks have to have a higher cash value or I haven't succeeded in my goal of putting more cash in my pocket."

Wendy observed, "And Georgia is making another good point to share with my friends. She talked about getting paid if the stock price goes up, but she didn't mention dividends, even though dividends also put cash in the Shareowner's pocket."

"Right," Georgia said. "As we discussed at the ranch, while dividends put cash in the Shareowner's pocket, they also take cash out of the company, and therefore reduce the company's Enterprise Value, dollar for dollar. When Enterprise Value goes down, stock price is not far behind."

Sam added, "In other words, dividends don't matter, unless by getting the cash out of the company, they preclude managers from making poor decisions, like overpaying for acquisitions or paying too high a price for share repurchases."

Sean then countered, "Whoa. In a perverse way, dividends do matter. There is an old corporate finance equation that demonstrates that the higher the dividend as a percent of net income, the lower the growth rate of the company, *unless the company increases its leverage (the ratio of debt to equity)*. The equation shows that a company's maximum growth rate without increasing leverage is (1-dividend/earnings per share) x return on equity."

Sean gave an example. "Assume that a company is generating a twenty percent return on Shareowners' book equity (ROE). If its dividend is $0.50 based on $2.00 of EPS, then its maximum growth rate is (1 - $0.50/$2.00) x 20%, or 15%. If the dividend is increased to $1.00, then the growth rate slows to (1 - $1.00/$2.00) x 20%, or 10%."

"You're right," said Sam. He shook his head. "It makes a person wonder about the wisdom of national tax policies that encourage dividend payouts at the expense of corporate growth and higher leverage."

Georgia let these ideas sink in while she took a bite of biscuit, savored its buttery flavor, and washed it down with orange juice. She was having fun being the center of this discussion and enjoyed keeping her audience on the edge of their chairs.

Wendy looked frustrated. "Georgia, so far, I think that you have told me to buy low and sell high."

"No," Georgia laughed. "I've told you that we are going to measure investment success using cash, not accounting numbers. *Now* I'm going to teach you how to buy cash cheap and sell it, dear."

"How do you do that?" asked Wendy.

"Easy," replied Georgia. "You have to start by learning how to measure cash."

8

A Company's Two Cash Values

Wendy looked confused. "What's so hard about measuring cash?"

"Well, it becomes confusing when you realize that *every company has two cash values*," replied Georgia.

Wendy's confusion turned to frustration; she turned and saw Sam grinning at her. She surrendered as Sam chuckled and said to Georgia, "OK, my friend, you're pressing your luck. Explain what you mean."

Georgia smiled and said, "I believe in the power of cash. I don't believe in alchemy. To me, accounting has become a distraction where college boys and college girls keep changing the rules and then trying to use alchemy to magically transform numbers on a piece of paper into cash. But their potions can't create cash where there is none, and none of their numbers tell me the real value of a company. So, Tom and I asked Sam for help in setting up the investing equivalent of the Texas Rangers, so that we could fend for ourselves until the cavalry arrived."

As Georgia paused, Wendy said, "Okay, you're saying that there is no magic that can turn numbers from a GAAP accounting, math model into hard, cold cash. So, what two cash values of a company are you 'Value Rangers' measuring?"

"That's easy," Georgia replied. "*The first cash value is the price of the company's stock that is quoted every day on the stock exchange.*"

To emphasize her point, Georgia sketched a company's first cash value on a page from Wendy's legal pad and said, "If a company's stock price is $150, then the company's first cash value is $150."

```
┌─────────────────────────────────────────────────────────────┐
│                                                               │
│      Company's                                                │
│        First            =              Stock Price            │
│      Cash Value                                               │
│                                                               │
└─────────────────────────────────────────────────────────────┘
```

"OK," said Wendy. "That's easy. What's the second cash value?"

Georgia responded, "*We call it the Enterprise Value. It is the present value of all the cash that the company currently has or will have in the future minus the company's current debt.* Your friends can think of it this way. Every asset owned by a company is used to create cash either now or in the future, either by producing products and services or by selling the asset if it is no longer needed. If you add up the present value of all the current and future cash and use part of the cash to pay off all the current debt, the cash that remains is what belongs to Shareowners—it's the Enterprise Value. If a dollar of cash is worth a dollar of cash, then this is the real value of a company. This is the second cash value of a company."

Georgia sketched a company's second cash value as follows:

```
┌─────────────────────────────────────────────────────────────┐
│                                                               │
│  Company's                                                    │
│   Second      = Current Cash  -   Current  +  Present Value of all │
│  Cash Value                        Debt      Future Free Cash Flow │
│   (OR                                                         │
│  Enterprise                                                   │
│   Value)                                                      │
│                                                               │
└─────────────────────────────────────────────────────────────┘
```

"Let me say it another way," said Wendy. "As we discussed at the ranch, the Enterprise Value of the company is the present value of all the free cash flow that the company generates through earnings and operations over its life. It's the *present value of the cash that is not needed for growth and which could freely be returned to Shareowners.* The value today, present value, of the 'free' cash in the company depends on *when* the cash is available to be paid out of the company. For example, $1 of cash in the company today has a value in the present, i.e., a present value, of $1. On the other hand, cash that is only available to the company when it earns it one year from now is only worth $0.91 to me today, therefore its present value is $0.91. The reason for this is that I need to earn a cash return of 10 percent, or $0.09, to justify the risk of owning the stock for a year while I wait to collect the $1.'"

"Right," said Georgia.

Wendy sketched an example of a company that currently had $100 in cash, had $50 in current debt, and was going to generate $100 per year in free cash flow every year into the future, which could be returned to Shareowners or reinvested in *new* projects in the company. She also assumed that the company had issued ten shares to Shareowners. Wendy said, "This sketch shows how the Enterprise Value of a company can be calculated using a picture of the cash flow that we call a 'cash-flow diagram.'

"The first column, called 'Present Value of Cash,' shows the current, or 'present value,' of the cash in any given row. The sum of this column is the Enterprise Value. In this case, the Enterprise Value is $1050."

"The Company's *Second* Cash Value is called Enterprise Value and can be depicted using a 'cash-flow diagram.'"

	Present Value of Cash **	Beginning of Year 1, i.e., now	Cash-Flow Diagram *								
			Cash Flow at the End of Year:								
			1	2	3	4	5	6	7	8	
Current Cash	$100	100									
− Current Debt	(50)	(50)									
+ Future Free Cash Flow	1,000	−	100	100	100	100	100	100	100	100	etc.
Enterprise Value	$1,050	50	100	100	100	100	100	100	100	100	etc.

* The cash-flow diagram is used to help people to visualize 'free cash flow'; it is a 'picture' of free cash flow. Positive numbers represent free cash inflow. Negative numbers represent free cash outflow to pay off debt or to invest in something.
* *The Present Value (PV) is calculated assuming a 10 percent desired return.

"Looks good," said Sean, "but notice that if you divide the company's $1,050 Enterprise Value by the 10 outstanding shares, the company has an Enterprise Value per share of $105, which is $45 less than the $150 stock price."

"Now we have *two* different cash values for the company," said Wendy as she turned toward Georgia. "Which one is right?"

Georgia smiled and said, "Like water, all cash seeks its own level. The only number that's right is the one that puts cash in my pocket."

Wendy's face went blank and Sean laughed.

Georgia chuckled.

9

Cash Seeks Its Own Level

From the look on Wendy's face, Georgia knew that she had better explain the relationship of these two cash values in a hurry or she would be toast—burned toast.

Georgia commenced her explanation. "As you observed, Wendy, I now have two cash numbers—the stock price and the Enterprise Value."

Wendy nodded as Sam smiled at her frustration. Georgia ignored them as she continued. "Let's talk about these numbers:

- We know that the *stock price* will fluctuate for many reasons. But *stock price is the tool that the Shareowner, uses to either make or destroy cash by virtue of the price at which he buys or sells the stock relative to the Enterprise Value.*

- We also know that the Enterprise Value will change, but its changes occur more slowly and are due to increases or decreases in the cash flow inside the company. *This cash number is controlled by what the company's management does to create (or destroy) cash inside the company over time."*

Georgia continued, "Obviously, I want to compare the stock price to the Enterprise Value per share to see if they are equal. Since a dollar of cash is worth a dollar of cash, these two numbers should be equal. As I said earlier, why would anyone pay more—or less—than a dollar for a dollar?"

"So," said Wendy, "if I wanted to explain it to my friends, I could do so like this:

Stock Price	**=**	**Company's Enterprise Value Per Share**

"And since I am comparing the company's stock price to the company's Enterprise Value, I would divide the company's total Enterprise Value by the number of outstanding shares to get the company's Enterprise Value *per share*. This is similar to the way we divide a company's total Net Income to get Earnings per share. The context tells my friends whether to use Enterprise Value or Enterprise Value *per share* for comparisons."

"You got it," said Georgia. "But," she continued, "as we discussed at the ranch last summer, the stock price and Enterprise Value are almost never equal."

Wendy put a second sketch on the table, saying, "This should be a good depiction of the additional factor that explains why they aren't equal—supply and demand for the stock."

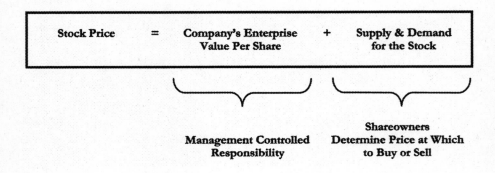

"Right," said Georgia. "And as you remember from the ranch, there is reliable data that demonstrates that approximately fifty percent of a company's stock price is determined by Enterprise Value and the remaining fifty percent by supply & demand factors."[22]

Sam interjected, "As an aside, the same data indicated that earnings per share (EPS) is only correlated eighteen percent with share price movement. In other words, Enterprise Value is over 175 percent, almost 2 times, more powerful than EPS in either predicting or determining stock price."

As Georgia reached for Wendy's legal pad, she said, "Wendy, here's something that helped me to understand how a company's two cash values change over time."

Georgia drew a graph as she explained, "Enterprise Value is the more stable of the two cash values because it is determined by employees' efforts to grow free cash flow over a long time. If managers are doing their jobs, Enterprise Value should increase fairly steadily over a long period of time. On the other hand, stock price can change pretty fast due to anything from an analyst's stock recommendation to world events."

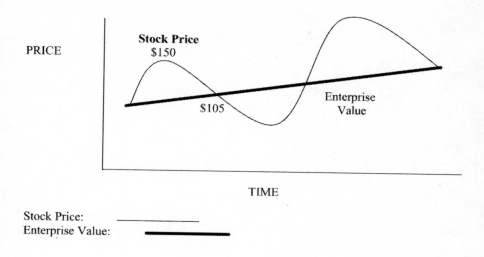

Georgia concluded, "If you believe that water seeks its own level and, therefore, that $1 of cash is worth $1 of cash, here is where the investing opportunity lies. If the stock price and the Enterprise Value are not equal, then one of them has to change to bring them closer to equilibrium. For example, if the stock price is *below* the Enterprise Value, then over time, the stock price should rise and put cash into my pocket. On the other hand, it the stock price is *above* the company's Enterprise Value, the stock price should fall and take cash out of my pocket. Pretty simple."

Sean urged her to give an example in terms of a single share of stock.

Georgia obliged, and as she did, she wrote the words "buy" and "sell" on the graph. "Let's assume that the stock price is $150 and the Enterprise Value is $105. Since the Enterprise Value is the more stable number, the stock price should fall toward $105 in order to bring the two cash values of the company into equilibrium."

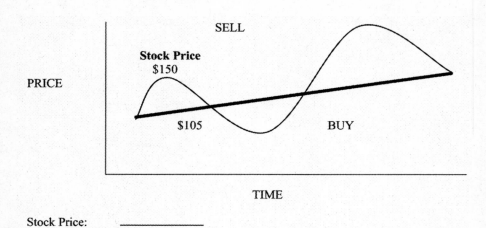

PRICE

Stock Price: _____

Enterprise Value: ▬▬▬▬▬▬▬

Georgia pointed respectively below then above the Enterprise Value Line as she said, "The Shareowner should buy when the stock price is below Enterprise Value and sell when the stock price is above Enterprise Value."

Georgia turned to Sam and asked, "Did I get that right?"

"Like a pro," he replied.

"Okay," said Wendy, "but, my friends, and investors in general, don't know a company's Enterprise Value. How can they determine if the stock price is above or below the Enterprise Value?"

10

My Money Ain't Free!

"You're right," said Georgia. "The accountants make it difficult for the average Shareowner to compute Enterprise Value. Let me share a few of my frustrations, then I'll show you how I estimate whether a stock price is above or below the Enterprise Value."

"Good enough," said Wendy.

"Conceptually, *calculating the Enterprise Value of a company involves two numbers,*" said Georgia. "The first set of numbers is the free-cash-flow forecast into the future. *Since my money ain't free, the second number is the rate of return that I need to earn on my investment in the company.* That is the 'interest rate' or 'discount rate' that I use to discount the company's cash flows to the present value. And, of course, the present value of the cash flows is the Enterprise Value."

Georgia continued, "The best way to get a good estimate of a company's Enterprise Value is for the accountants to add a fourth Valuation Statement [1], like Sam presented at the ranch last summer. It would give Shareowners easily accessible free cash flows and present them transparently so that an investor could estimate Enterprise Value. But even with the cash flows, the Shareowner needs to know what return he should expect to earn on his equity."

"OK," said Sean. "I see where you are going. You need a benchmark for the minimum rate of return that you should plan to earn on your stock investment."

"Right," said Georgia. "That *benchmark return is the rate that I need to earn in order justify holding this stock, rather than some other stock, until the future cash flow is earned.*"

"*But,*" she continued, "I need something practical. I don't want someone confusing the issue with a bunch of Greek letters like Alpha, Beta, and," she joked, "Zulu." For practical purposes, all stocks have the same risk. For example, no Greek letter, which implies that the stock was low risk, can make up my loss when 'low risk'—'low Beta'—utility stocks can go bankrupt in eighteen months

---

1.   Please see the Appendix.

because California won't let them pass the cost of electricity on to their customers."

"Okay," said Wendy. "I think this is a workable concept. Now, what return do you expect to earn on your equity?"

After taking a sip of coffee, Georgia looked up and replied, "Tom and I discussed what should be the benchmark for the return that our stocks should earn. We kept coming back to the simple idea that over the past seventy years—through recessions, depressions, wars, Democrats, Republicans, and 'boom' times—the Standard & Poors 500 has earned about eight percent above inflation.[23] Since the S&P is a diversified portfolio of 500 stocks, Tom and I figured that we should expect to earn at least inflation plus eight percent on any individual stock, or we ought to just buy the S&P 500 index. The return on the S&P 500 represents what Sam called the 'opportunity cost.' The opportunity cost is what we 'miss out on' if an individual stock doesn't earn at least what the S&P 500 earns."

"*So, your benchmark return is inflation plus eight percent,*" said Sean.

"Right," said Georgia. "That's the cash return that we expect to earn from any stock over three to five years, or we won't buy it or hold it. We also took a tip from Sam and decided to use the inflation rate that economists forecast for the next twelve months, plus or minus. If that isn't available, we use the inflation rate from the past year."

"So," continued Sean, "if inflation is projected at two percent, you expect a stock with a market value of $150 to earn ten percent. That's two percent inflation plus eight percent, or $15 in the next year, in order to equal or break even with what you could earn by just investing $150 in an S&P 500 index mutual fund."

"Yep," nodded Georgia, smiling. "You're pretty smart for a city boy."

They all laughed.

Finally, Wendy looked at Georgia and inquired, "Now, how do we make all this simple so my friends can use it to invest? How do you Value Rangers do it?"

11

Why Are CEOs Using Your Money for Free?

Georgia answered Wendy's question by saying, "To make investing simple for your friends, let's get them focused, like a laser. Ask them, *'Why are CEOs using your money for free?'*"

Wendy laughed and exclaimed, "That will get their attention."

Georgia continued, "If they need proof that CEOs are using their money for free, show them the income statement of any company that they are investing in. Show them that while the company pays for raw materials, labor, buildings, executive salaries and bonuses, interest expense, and even taxes for government services, *nowhere* does the company pay for equity. So, your friends have to conclude that CEOs are using their equity for free."

"I'm with you so far," said Wendy.

"Next, ask them how much CEOs should earn for them," said Georgia. "Your friends probably won't have a clear idea, so point out what the S&P 500 has earned historically—inflation plus eight percent. Tell them they shouldn't expect to earn less than that or they're giving away their money."

"Elaborate," said Wendy.

"Well," replied Georgia. "There are two points here. First, your friends need to expect to earn some return on their money, or it's free to the user. If their money is invested in a bond, there will be a contractual requirement to pay interest for its use. If they invest their money in stocks, they should expect to earn a long-run return at least equal to the return on the S&P 500—inflation plus eight percent. Second, if their equity investment only earns six percent, but the long-term S&P 500 return is ten percent, then your friends just gave away four percent each year on their investment. But they could be in for an even bigger surprise."

"How so?" asked Wendy.

"They could lose the 4%-per-annum difference all at once. Wendy, remind your friends that if they buy a stock at $150—a six-percent yield—when the Enterprise Value that yields ten percent is $105, then the odds are that your friends will loose $45, or about thirty percent, of their investment in the first year."

"Why is that?" asked Wendy.

Sam replied, "Like water seeking its own level, the market return always regresses to its long-term mean return, in this case ten percent. The reason is simple: if everyone wanted to earn ten percent, then no one would pay more than $105 for the stock—that's all the cash flows in the company are worth at a ten-percent return. If your friends have paid $150, then there is only one way that your friends can be rescued."

"How's that?" asked Wendy.

Georgia responded, "If there is a greater fool out there who is willing to pay, say $160, and accept an even lower rate of return than your friends will earn at a stock cost of $150."

Sean tilted his chair back and grinned at Wendy. Oh, how he loved her reaction to the Greater Fool Theory of Investing.

Wendy gave him a strained acknowledgment, and then turned to Georgia. "I think my friends will get the point. No one wants to be an obvious fool. So, this is all useful background, but I still don't see how my friends can tell if the stock price is above or below the Enterprise Value. Help me. What's next?"

Georgia replied, "OK, let's get to my quick fix. I call it 'Pay me now, or pay me later, BUT PAY ME.' Here's how it works.

"The company can pay me the ten percent in one of two ways—by earning the return today ('Pay me now') or by earning dollars in the future that equate to my required ten percent return in today's dollars ('Pay me later')," said Georgia.

"Makes sense," said Wendy. "Obviously, the return can be some combination of the two."

"Right." Georgia continued, "*Let's first check to see if the company is earning ten percent today. If not, I will learn how much I am depending on management to grow the company's free cash flow in the future to make up for the shortfall.*"

"Go ahead. I'm making a note," said Wendy.

Georgia paused and waited for Wendy to finish her note and then reached for the legal pad, saying, "Let me show you a neat way to calculate the 'Pay me now or pay me later' tradeoff."

As she spoke, Georgia wrote on the page. "First, we need to put our goal at the top of the page. We expect that the investment will produce our benchmark return of 10%, or we shouldn't buy the stock. If the current stock price is $150, then in dollar terms, the 10% target return equals $15 per year.

"Next, let's calculate what the stock is paying us right now. With a current stock price of $150 and an earnings per share (EPS) of $10, the stock is currently 'paying' Shareowners 6.66% ($10/$150).

"By subtracting the 6.66% from 10%, we see that the company is falling short of earning our target yield by 3.34% (or $5) per year. This shortfall is what must be paid to me later through growth in free cash flow.

Georgia paused and turned the pad around so that Wendy and Sean could absorb it.

Assumptions: Stock Price: $150

Earnings per share: $10

Benchmark return: 10%

PAY ME NOW:

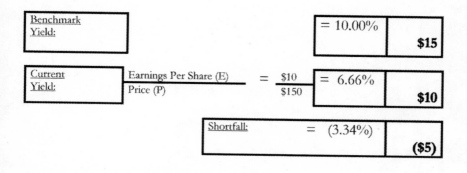

or, PAY ME LATER:

The 3.34%, or ($5), shortfall in EPS must be made up through future growth (G) of free cash flow.

After studying the pad, Wendy turned it back to Georgia and said, "Okay, now how can my friends estimate if the company can make up the 3.34% shortfall?"

Georgia replied, "Here's the neat solution that Sam and Sean developed. As I explain it, notice that there are only three things that I need to know:

> First, the stock's price (P)
> Second, the earnings per share (EPS)
> Third, the growth rate (G) of the company's free cash flow.

"All three of these are easy for the average person to find. The ratio of the stock price and earnings per share are available every day in the financial papers. While it is presented as the price-to-earnings (P/E) ratio, it is just the inverse of the way we compute the 'pay me now' yield (i.e., the E/P).

"Estimates of the company's cash-flow growth (G) are available from sources such as Value Line, which is available in the public library or online."

"OK," Wendy repeated impatiently, "I can tell my friends that their first step is to mentally fill in the 'pay me now or pay me later' table to see how much they are depending on future growth to justify the current stock price. And I can tell them to get the P/E ratio out of the newspaper and to get the estimated cash-flow growth rate from Value Line. But how do my friends use these two numbers to determine if the company has enough growth in future cash flow to cover the shortfall?"

12

The Value of Growth Is Limited

"Well," replied Georgia, "As I said earlier, forecasting and discounting growth of cash flows is impossible given the time and information available to busy people like me. So, I asked Sam to come up with a simple way for me to tell if the current price of the stock is below (a buy signal) or above (a sell signal) a company's Enterprise Value. To do that, Sam and Sean had to calculate the value of growth that is included in any given Enterprise Value. The reason is that *there is only so much that any given amount of future cash is worth in today's dollars.* After all, even growth has its limits. Trees don't grow to the sky."

Sam interrupted, "Before we go further, Georgia, remind us again what you mean by 'growth.'"

Georgia obliged. "Sam, as you have pointed out many times in the past, depending on whom you are talking to, growth is either the most misunderstood concept in corporate finance or the most abused for the purposes of selfish self-interest. In the context of what management controls, there is only one growth that matters to the Shareowner. That is growth of Enterprise Value, the net present value of future free cash flow."

"Absolutely right," seconded Sean. "Growth in sales, growth through acquisitions, growth of the return on the equity on the GAAP financial statements, e.g., Return on Equity, Return on Capital Employed, do not produce any value for the Shareowner unless the Enterprise Value *also* increases.[24] Growth in things like sales and acquisitions include cash that belongs to others, such as suppliers and employees. The growth in cash that must be paid out to others, like suppliers and employees, doesn't create value for Shareowners unless it accompanies increases (growth) in the present value of cash which can be returned to Shareowners—Enterprise Value."

Sam observed, "Since share price is 175 percent more highly correlated with Enterprise Value than earnings per share, we ought to pay management for growing Enterprise Value rather than EPS, using the techniques discussed at the ranch last summer."

Wendy refocused the conversation to mechanics. "Okay, Georgia, explain how your Value Rangers came up with a shortcut to compare the current stock price to the Enterprise Value to see if the stock was over or undervalued."

"Glad to," Georgia replied. "Our tool is a simple table that determines if a company is currently earning its cost of capital. If it isn't, then we can check to see if the company's anticipated future growth is large enough to cover the current shortfall in earning its cost of capital."

"OK," said Wendy. "Just go through it slowly so that I can explain it to my friends."

Georgia nodded and began by opening her wallet to retrieve a laminated card. She unfolded the card so that Wendy could see it as she explained.

The 'PEG' Ratio
for a 10% return

Current P/E (1)	'Pay me now,' Current Yield to Shareowners implied by Current P/E (2)	'Or pay me later,' Minimum Annual Growth Rate for 10 years (% p.a.) Required to justify P/E by making up Current Yield Shortfall. (3)	P/E / G Ratio (4) 'But pay me!' Maximum Price/Earnings-to-Growth-Rate ('PEG') Ratio Required to earn 10%	Reality Check Column (5) Size of Company Sales in 10 years if grown at Minimum Annual Growth Rate. (Starting from $1mm.)
10	10%	0%	-	$1.0
13	7.7	5	2.6	1.6
17	5.9	10	1.7	2.6
21	4.8	15	1.4	4.0
28	3.6	20	1.4	6.2
38	2.6	25	1.5	9.3
51	2.0	30	1.7	13.8
68	1.5	35	1.9	20.1
92	1.1	40	2.3	28.9
122	0.8	45	2.7	41.1
163	0.6	50	3.3	57.7

Acquisitions do NOT add growth, because the present value of their free cash flow is usually paid away in the purchase price.

"The first two columns of the table are used to determine if the company is earning my ten percent benchmark cost of equity (two percent inflation plus eight percent). For example, when I read the financial section of the newspaper, I can get the P/E ratio and stock price. If the P/E ratio is 15, then, by using interpolation, I enter the first column of the table using a 15 P/E. Then, I can look at the second column, the 'Pay me now' column, to see that the company is only earning 6.6% out of the 10% return that I want to earn. The third column, 'Or pay me later,' then shows the MINIMUM annual growth that the company must achieve in order to make up the shortfall of 3.4% between my 10% desired return and the 6.6% return it currently produces.

Georgia continued, "Another way to think of this is that if you knew the stock price is $150 and the EPS is $10, then by dividing the earnings by the price, we determine that the company is earning 6.66%. Using the 6.66%, you could then enter the table through the second column."

Wendy interjected, *"So, the higher the P/E ratio, the more that the Shareowner must depend on the company's future growth to make up the shortfall versus the 10% target.* As long as you believe that the company's cash flow will grow faster than the number in the 'Or, pay me later' (third) column, there is a high probability of earning your 10%."

"Right," replied Georgia.

Wendy asked, "So, why do you need the fourth column, called 'BUT, Pay me'?"

Georgia replied, "I use the PEG ratio for two reasons. First, it is a constant reminder that there is a specific, quantifiable tradeoff between growth and current return. It reminds me that there is no alchemy. The cash has to be here now or in the future, and the future cash has a known value in today's dollars. Second, if I don't have the 'PEG' table with me when I am reading P/E ratios in a newspaper, I make the assumption that I won't buy a stock unless the PEG ratio is below 1, or maybe 1.25. That way I can screen stocks on the run and then research those that meet my PEG test when I get time. If I could remember the P/E and growth columns, I wouldn't really need the PEG column itself."

"Fine," said Wendy. "Can you give me a little more background on how the table was developed, in case my friends ask?"

Georgia turned to Sean and said, "Sean, since you developed the model, why don't you give Wendy a brief explanation of how it works?"

13

Dancing with PEG

Sean picked up the card and held it so that others could see it as he enthusiastically said, "I love dancing with Peg."

Other than a "you really didn't say that" stare from Wendy, his audience was stoic.

Sean laughed and continued. "The 'PEG card' shows 'rule of thumb' relationships between price-to-earnings (P/E) ratios and free cash flow 'growth rates' based upon a series of sensitivities completed using my basic Enterprise Value model [1]. *These growth rates are the growth rate of a company's annual free cash flow. The growth rates exclude acquisitions* because in most cases the acquisition price usually equals or exceeds the present value of the acquired free cash flows, including 'synergies,' and therefore adds no value to the acquirer's stock. Instead of P/Es, it would have been better to use something closer to cash-flow ratios such as Price to Earnings Before Interest, Taxes, and Amortization—P/EBITA. However, P/Es provide a useful 'rule of thumb,' because most people have easy access to current P/Es; since goodwill, except in the event of impairment, is now excluded as an expense on the income statement, earnings are a somewhat closer approximation to free cash flow."

"What are the key assumptions in these numbers, and how do you use them?" asked Wendy.

Sean responded, "In developing this PEG table, the model assumes a constant growth rate in annual free cash flow for ten years and then no growth thereafter. I stop growth at ten years because companies usually have to make major invest-

---

1. The Enterprise Value model takes the forecast free cash flows and discounts them to the present value using a discount rate equal to the weighted cost of the company's debt and equity capital. (This weighted discount rate is called the company's weighted average cost of capital or 'WACC'.) The net amount of a company's current cash minus current debt is then added to the present value of free cash flows to obtain the Enterprise Value.

ments to reinvent their products in order to grow the whole company at high rates beyond that period. Every company is different. *My chart works for the vast majority of companies,* but you always have to use some judgment in the application of any model or rule of thumb."

"Georgia explained the columns pretty well except for the final column," he continued. *The final column is a reality check.* It shows how big the company would be after ten years if it grew at the designated growth rate. For example, if the company's current sales were $1 billion, with a P/E of 92, the implied growth rate of 40% per annum means that sales would need to be $28.9 billion *(excluding acquisitions)* in ten years in order to justify the current stock price. The column is another way to cause you to ask, 'Is that realistic?'"

Sean continued, "Assuming that one-time events, such as charge-offs of closed plants or costs associated with staff reductions, are not distorting earnings, comparing the implied growth rate to the historic growth rate tells me a lot. For example, if a company has a sixty percent market share in a market growing ten percent per year, an implied P/E growth rate of twenty-five percent is unrealistic. The company would have 100 percent market share and outgrow the market in five years. Their competition isn't going to abandon the market, especially if margins and growth are high. Therefore, with extremely high probability, the company's stock is overvalued. It is highly likely that competition will force the entire industry to reduce margins as they attempt to take market share."

Sean looked at Wendy. "Also, if the company's implied P/E growth rate is materially above its historic growth rate and nothing has changed, it is likely that the stock is being traded by momentum investors and is not trading based upon its fundamental Enterprise Value."

"What's wrong with a stock trading based on momentum?" asked Wendy.

"Nothing," replied Sean, "so long as the investor recognizes that's how it's trading and recognizes how vulnerable the price is. The higher a stock price is above the Enterprise Value, the higher the probability and magnitude of a market decline. As you know, Sam and I have a name for investing in stocks which trade at the excessively high growth rates implied by these high P/Es."

Wendy lowered her head, shook it slowly, and with humor in her eyes and a smile, said, "Yes, yes, I know, *the 'Greater Fool Theory of Investing.'*"

The table broke out in laughter, and Sean said, "Right on, Wendy. I knew you were a secret admirer."

Sean concluded, "When growth rates implied by the P/E are unrealistically high, the only way for a Shareowner to realize value is to find a greater fool to buy the stock at an even higher P/E, and, therefore, an even higher implied growth rate, or lower return. In the absence of that greater fool, eventually the stock price will fall, or regress, to the company's Enterprise Value, which yields the ten percent return. As we discussed, that can be a long fall for a 100 P/E stock."

"And," said Georgia, "it means that the last buyer at the highest price, and therefore the highest P/E, is the Greatest Fool."

Sean and Sam gave her a round of applause.

"Thanks for the explanation," Wendy said, laughing. "The PEG table seems easy enough to understand. But, Georgia, show us a little more about how it works so that I am sure that I can explain it to my friends."

Georgia responded, "It's pretty simple. One way to do it is to take the P/E out of the newspaper. I like to do a little more. I get the company's current stock price (P). Then I look at both the past twelve-months' earnings (E) and the forecast twelve-months' earnings. I can get the forecast earnings online from my brokers or from a source such as Value Line. I like to calculate the P/E and PEG ratios using both the past twelve months' (trailing) and next twelve months' (forecast) earnings as a means of double checking what is going on. I usually prefer to buy based on the ratios calculated using the trailing earnings number."

Georgia continued, "The final piece is the forecast growth rate of free cash flow (G). I usually pull this estimate out of Value Line. I then compute the PEG ratio and compare it to the maximum PEG ratio in the table. The maximum ratio represents the maximum price that I should pay for the stock if I want to earn a ten percent benchmark return—two percent inflation plus eight percent."

"For example," said Georgia, "if the stock price (P) is $100, earnings (E) are $5, and the company's cash flow has no growth, then I wouldn't buy the stock. It's only earning five percent for me. I don't even need the table to tell me that I wouldn't pay more than $50 for the stock if it was only earning $5 with no growth, and I wanted to earn 10%."

"Now, continued Georgia, "Let me give two other examples. First, a stock with a price of $130, earnings of $10 (P/E of 13) and a growth rate of 5% (PEG of 2.6 or 13/5). Since it is equal to the maximum PEG of 2.6 required to earn a 10% yield, I might probably buy the stock, but NOT above $130.

"Let's look at a second stock, with a price of $200, earnings of $5 (P/E of 40) and a growth rate of 20%. The PEG is two (40/20). By going to the table and using a little interpolation, I can determine that at the stock's 40 P/E, the maximum PEG that would let me earn 10%, is about 1.5. Therefore, I would NOT buy the stock. With a little more work, by computing backward from a 1.5 PEG and earnings of $5, I could determine that the most that I could pay for this stock and still earn 10% is $150. In other words, I wouldn't buy it at a P/E above 30."

Georgia concluded, "I am pretty conservative because of the potential for earnings, or other, surprises, so I usually try to buy stocks when the PEG is around 1.0 and both cash flow and earnings are forecast to grow. I want to emphasize that even before I use the PEG table, I do my homework to determine if the company is going to stay in business, and I always diversify my investments. No technique is foolproof. There are always surprises."

Sam added an observation. "Let me emphasize something that Sean said. In theory, we ought to be looking at growth in free cash flow after tax relative to the stock price. But, until the accounting industry gives the average investor a user-friendly tool like the Valuation Statement to present the needed data, we must work with approximations that give the average investor the ability to take care of himself. Now that Financial Accounting Standard 142, which covers accounting for goodwill, excludes unimpaired acquisition goodwill as an expense from the income statement, EPS is closer to a cash-flow number; therefore, it can be used for estimates."

"How do you treat 'one-time' or 'non-recurring' charges that reduce EPS?" questioned Wendy.

"Simple," said Georgia. "If it's cash out of my Shareowner's pocket, it's a cost and reduces earnings (E)."

Sam endorsed Georgia's comment. "In the absence of detailed, transparent information presented in the form of the Valuation Statement, the investor should assume that the one-time charges are costs of doing business, and therefore reduce Enterprise Value. In the current environment, it is almost illogical to assume otherwise. One-time or non-recurring charges represent real cash out of the Shareowner's pocket regardless of the reason. This is especially true of companies that are 'serial' chargers of non-recurring items. For example, through December 2002, Motorola had fifteen consecutive quarters in which it had 'non-recurring' charges.[25] That comes out of the Shareowner's pocket no matter how management or the accountants characterize it."

Wendy interrupted, "But Sam, what about one-time *non-cash* charges, such as goodwill write-offs (impairment), when it is determined that an acquisition is not worth the original purchase price?"

Sam laughed. "Wendy, goodwill write-offs are cash charges. It's just a question of timing as to when the cash actually leaves the Shareowner's pocket. The cash usually leaves the Shareowner's pocket at the time of the acquisition, or through the decline in the acquirer's stock price soon after the acquisition. After all, *at some point, cash equal to the charge was paid out, or there wouldn't be a charge. That cash payout reduces the cash in the Shareowner's pocket.*"

Sam concluded with a note of empathy. "Again, Wendy, because this PEG technique is a rule of thumb used on a variety of companies, it is not mathematically precise for an individual company, but it is close enough to be functional. If this technique had been used by investors, it would have helped millions of people avoid the losses on individual bombs like Enron, WorldCom, Global Crossing, Quest, and AOL Time Warner as well as the dot-com, telecom, and late 90s stock market bubbles."

"I get the point," conceded Wendy.

Georgia concluded, "But in the end, I think that the accountants need to get with it and give us a GAAP Valuation Statement. It would be more accurate and even more reliable than our PEG table."

"Right on," seconded Sean.

Then, with a wry smile, Georgia turned to Sam and said, "I guess all of this just proves the point that cash is king."

Sam nodded with a smile.

Then, the foursome sat in silence. Finally, Wendy said, "Sam, when we began last evening, I asked for your help on three topics. First, to help my friends eliminate distractions; second, to give them a benchmark to determine a fair price for a stock; and, third, to identify the true cause of the crisis in corporate responsibility. Together, we have answered the first two questions in a grand manner. But, in a larger context, our answers feel like a 'quick fix.' Is there a 'root cause' of and solution to the crisis in corporate responsibility?"

PART IV

The Cause...
and Solution

14

When Fidelity Is Infidelity

Sam took up Wendy's challenge and got straight to the point. *"Actions follow measurement and pay."*

"The cause of the 'crisis in corporate responsibility' is that generally accepted accounting principles (GAAP) consider Shareowner capital to be free. As a result, we are measuring and paying people to do the wrong thing. American companies are paying managers to create GAAP earnings per share by *arbitraging* historic numbers without any regard for the amount of equity capital that they use in the process. In effect, we are measuring the wrong thing using a rubber yardstick. As a result, management is often earning incentives to destroy economic value. *Fidelity to GAAP has become infidelity to the Shareowner and to society."*

"How can accurate accounting be unfaithful to Shareowners?" challenged Wendy.

"Faithfulness to the GAAP measurement system is mandatory. The problem is that the GAAP measurement system is *not* faithful either to the Shareowner's objective of earning the cost of his capital or to society's goal of raising living standards through effective allocation of capital," replied Sam.

Wendy challenged Sam again. "OK, I accept your point that GAAP is not faithful to the Shareowner, but explain further how it is unfaithful to society."

Sam replied, "Nations charter companies in order to create vehicles that can raise large amounts of capital and take risks beyond the capabilities of a single individual. But society's objective is not just to raise large amounts of money or to spread risk. *Society's objective is to have companies create economic value so that citizens will have a better standard of living and greater economic freedom to realize their individual potential."*

Sam observed, "And how do companies create economic value? Well, in this regard, the objectives of society and the Shareowner are identical. *Whether creating economic value for society or for individual Shareowners, it is accomplished when companies invest capital effectively. That is evidenced when a company earns more than its cost of capital and increases that return year after year.* That's plain logic and Economics 101. Note: Economics 101, *not* Accounting 101, economics being where cash flow is compared to cash invested."

He continued, "For GAAP to faithfully measure economic value, GAAP needs to incorporate a fourth financial statement, a Valuation Statement. Once this transparent Valuation Statement is available, the free capital markets can then decide the best financial statement by which to judge a company's performance and price its stock."

Sam continued, "While there will always be greedy people and people who break laws, the crisis in corporate responsibility wasn't caused by greedy, bad people. Executives and directors aren't bad people. They are doing what society is measuring and paying them to do, to create accounting EPS regardless of the amount of equity used. We gave them the wrong measure, and in addition, we put it within their power to adjust the measuring stick. That's our fault. We must fix it."

"Can you explain that differently so my friends can better understand the point?" asked Wendy.

"Sure," replied Sam. "Let me share four lessons that we learned from the quality process that may help them to see why measurement and pay are at the heart of the crisis in corporate responsibility.

"The quality process taught us the following:

- *The best way to eliminate defects is to prevent them. Prevention is accomplished by correcting the defective process* rather than by reworking defective products.

- *A bad 'incapable' process produces defects even when capable, well-intentioned people operate it.* The problem is the process, not the people.

- *To correct the defective process, the process must be measured.* To eliminate the defects the defective process attribute must be measured and corrected. If you measure and correct the wrong attribute, e.g. length instead of width, then the process will still produce defects.

- *What gets measured gets done. Without measures and accountability, there is no continuity over time.* People lose sight of the solution due to 'more urgent,' new priorities."

Sam continued, "As a society, we are producing defective products: companies that are destroying economic value. To correct the defective GAAP measurement process, we must measure the right attribute and then pay management based upon that new measure. Wendy, *the solution to the crisis in corporate responsibility is to change GAAP accounting so that we measure corporations on whether they are creating Enterprise Value and to pay people based upon that measure.* From a mechanical perspective, the place to start is to add a Valuation Statement to GAAP financial reporting."

Sean volunteered, "Sam, that sounds like our earlier point. Chicken wire, in the form of new laws, regulations, and 'perp' walks, isn't going to keep the bears away from the raw meat. Chicken wire just makes a mess that we have to clean up after the bear gets to the meat. The real solution is to refocus the bear's motivation so that all of his energy is directed toward getting to the honey instead of the raw meat."

Sam nodded. "That's the bottom line. By changing how people are measured and by paying them based on the new measure, they will stop doing the 'bad' things associated with the old measure, because there's no reward in it."

Wendy then chimed in. "Sam, how do we get companies and accountants to give us a Valuation Statement?"

"The same way that we got them to give us quality cars," he replied.

"How's that?" asked Wendy.

Sam replied, "Treat stock conceptually as if it were a consumer product. Don't buy the stock if it doesn't have a label; demand a Valuation Statement as if it were a food label on a soup can or a warning label on a cigarette pack. Get consumers and institutional investors to advocate the Valuation Statement at annual meetings, in letters to CEOs, in letters to public auditors and to the Securities and Exchange Commission. If companies don't provide Valuation Statements, refuse to buy their product, i.e. their stock. Vote out company auditors who don't support the Valuation Statement. Get the press to write stories about companies that do provide Valuation Statements—and those that don't.

Sam continued, "It took us a few years, but we finally got quality cars. We can do it with stock."

Wendy nodded as Georgia mimed applause.

After pausing for a moment, Sam summarized. "Wendy, *while the root cause of the corporate crisis is that GAAP considers Shareowners' capital to be free, we need to put it in a broader context.*

"There is an ongoing national failure in corporate governance. It is the failure of generally accepted accounting principles to measure the creation (or destruction) of economic value (Enterprise Value) in companies. The national solution is to incorporate a Valuation Statement into generally accepted accounting principles

(GAAP), including the current cost of Shareowners' capital as a cost of doing business."

Wendy and Sean considered this, then nodded thoughtfully in agreement.

Sean added, "As you said, Sam, the quality process taught us that if you measure the wrong thing, you produce defects. Corporate directors are measuring the wrong thing."

15

Needed: An Effectiveness Revolution

What the superior man seeks,
is in himself.
What the inferior man seeks,
is in others.

—Confucius, *Stock Trader's Almanac: 2003*

After a few moments, Georgia volunteered, "Sam, *we need an Effectiveness Revolution.*"

"A what?" asked Wendy. "What's that?"

"Let me try this one," offered Sam. "*The quality process, the Internet, and the PC were essentially an efficiency revolution. They helped us to increase productivity by 'doing things right.'* We learned benchmarking, through which the vast majority of companies improved quality and reduced costs. But, by definition, at some point what was once 'world class' became the norm, and companies and countries eventually benchmarked themselves into efficient mediocrity—they have trouble distinguishing their value added versus other companies and countries. Sometimes they become world class at efficiently doing unnecessary things.

"*As a society, we need to change our business culture.* Business culture is changed through leadership, measurement, and incentives, *not* just good intentions. It is time to forgo incremental thinking and make a quantum leap that spawns an Effectiveness Revolution focused on 'doing the right things.' Doing the right things in an economic context means doing things that earn more than the cost of capital invested. It also means avoiding or preventing doing things that destroy Enterprise Value."

Sam concluded, "It is especially important to America that we make this change now. The world is going through the second phase of Globalization.[26] In the first phase, manufacturing—blue-collar—jobs moved, and are still moving, offshore to developing countries. In the second phase of Globalization, cheap, reliable communications technology has made it possible for white-collar jobs, such as accounting, chip design, engineering, architecture, and financial analysis, to move offshore to developing countries, where labor is less than fifty percent the cost in the U.S. If developed countries are to maintain their standard of living and coincident economic freedom for their people, they must move up the value-added chain. To do that, they must focus people on making the right decisions the first time, decisions that create rather than destroy economic value. For example, as a society we cannot afford to waste precious resources putting together acquisitions that seventy percent of the time put people out of productive jobs and destroy economic value for Shareowners. And as a nation, we cannot afford unnecessary regulations based on the wrong measures that make free enterprise less effective. We need minimal regulations on the right measures. *The most important thing that America can do to move up the value-added chain is to put a measurement system in place that measures the creation of economic (cash) value and then to implement incentives for people to create it.*"

Georgia observed, "Sam, imagine if the hundreds of billions of dollars of Enterprise Value destroyed annually by unnecessary acquisitions had been invested in research to create new products. We might have developed cures for cancer and heart disease, or hydrogen cars to reduce energy consumption and pollution, and in the process, created value for Shareowners and society."

Sam replied, "I firmly believe that the failure of GAAP to measure the creation of economic value in enterprises has cost our society a terrible price. We have trained people to be managers, investment bankers, analysts, accountants, and lawyers to do unproductive acquisitions and arbitrage GAAP accounting instead of being scientists and engineers discovering new ideas or creating new products. Over the past fifty years, the failure of GAAP measurement to focus business on doing the 'right things' to create Enterprise Value has effectively lost years of research and the economic growth associated with it.

There was a pause in the conversation, until Sean added, "You know, a Valuation Statement, which measures and makes Enterprise Value more transparent, should dampen stock market volatility and make our capital markets more efficient. And that should lead to fewer stock market bubbles, and therefore, to less economic disruption on Main Street."

"How so?" asked Wendy.

Sean replied, "If a Valuation Statement gave investors a transparent way to estimate the Enterprise Value, they would be less prone to pay excessive prices for stocks under The Greater Fool Theory of Investing."

"I like it," Georgia said, laughing.

After a pause, the group turned toward Sam as he said, "Enterprise measurement and compensation will be the next phase of national competitive advantage. How we measure and motivate people dictates not only our national business culture and its ability to create value, but also our standard of living, and hence our economic freedom. We cannot leave it up to the accounting industry any longer; too much is at stake. In the world of global business, if a nation is not best in class in enterprise measurement and motivation, it cannot be best in class in creating economic freedom for its citizens. For the sake of future generations, we must focus people on the creation of economic value (Enterprise Value). We need an Effectiveness Revolution to focus us on doing the right things the first time."

With that, the small group of friends became pensive. During the next fifteen minutes they finished their coffee over small talk.

16

On the Road Again

After Wendy and Sean left the Cracker Barrel, Sam and Georgia waited for Georgia's husband, Tom, to bring the eighteen-wheeler back with its load. When he arrived, he exchanged warm greetings with Sam, had a quick cup of coffee, and went out to get the rig.

Sam and Georgia waited in the vestibule.

When the rig pulled up, Georgia grabbed Sam's arm tightly and held close to him as he escorted her to the truck.

As they walked, she confided, "Sam, you know I can take care of Tom and me by using the PEG table to decide how to invest in stocks. But I am scared for my grandchildren. You were right on when you said that as a nation, the only way we can have greater economic freedom and let our grandchildren realize their individual potential is to create economic value. Sam, for the sake of our children and grandchildren, we have to change the way that companies and managers are measured and paid."

Georgia gave Sam a hug and kiss on the cheek and climbed up into the rig.

Sam waved to Tom and Georgia as they pulled away. He walked over to his Durango and climbed aboard.

Free enterprise was on the road again.

17

In Good Company

The fire crackled and gave a warm glow to the ST Bar's Great Room as Sam sat quietly reading and occasionally reflecting on the past days' discussions. A passage in the book he was reading struck him as particularly relevant. The book was titled *Relativity: The Special and the General Theory.*[27] According to the preface, Albert Einstein wrote it to provide a clear explanation of the Theory of Relativity that anyone could understand. The particular passage related to why the theory hadn't been identified earlier. Einstein wrote:

> Geometry sets out from certain conceptions such as 'plane,' 'point,' and 'straight line,' with which we are able to associate more or less definitive ideas, and from certain simple propositions (axioms) which, in virtue of these ideas, we are inclined to accept as 'true.' Then, on the basis of a logical process, the justification of which we feel ourselves compelled to admit, all remaining propositions are shown to follow from those axioms, *i.e.* they are proven. A proposition is then correct ('true') when it has been derived in the recognized manner from the axioms. The question of the 'truth' of the individual geometric propositions is thus reduced to one of the 'truth' of the axioms.

Sam chuckled to himself as he reflected on the last sentence. He spoke out loud as he paraphrased it:

> The truth of a model's answer is ultimately a question of the truth of the assumptions on which it is built…a truism known by every good engineer.

He wondered if the accountants, directors, and others who used and regulated financial statements would ever admit that all GAAP accounting models were defective so long as they assumed that Shareowners' money was free.

Sam smiled, shook his head, and returned to Einstein's good company.

Glossary

Announcement Effect:	The term "announcement effect" is used to describe the sudden purchase or sale of a stock or bond as the result of an announcement. The announcement can be from analysts, the company, or a number of other sources. Price moves due to announcement effects usually overshoot the equilibrium price and correct toward equilibrium, which in the case of a stock is its Enterprise Value.
Brokerage, or Brokerage Company:	Brokerage companies facilitate the public's exchange of publicly-traded debt and equity. They also sell initial and new issues of debt and equity for companies.
Capital Markets:	Capital markets is the term used to describe the market for both public and private debt and equity instruments of all shapes and sizes.
Corporate Governance:	Corporate governance consists of the rules that a corporation uses to govern itself. Technically, these rules are contained in the company's articles of incorporation, by-laws, and the rules of organizations that regulate them, such as the Securities and Exchange Commission, and the rules of the stock exchange on which they list. Corporate governance encompasses, among other things, what Shareowners vote on, how directors are elected, how finances are reported, and how company employees are measured and paid.

Cost of Capital:	*Capital is comprised of debt capital and equity capital. Each has its own cost. The blended cost is called the weighted average cost of capital or "WACC."*
	For example: Assume that a company had $100 of debt, costing four percent after tax, and an equity market value of $300, costing 10%. (2% inflation plus 8%) The weighted average cost (WACC) of its $400 of capital is 8.5%, and is calculated as follows: $100/$400 x 4% plus $300/$400 x 10%.
Earnings (E):	*Earnings are the net income of the company, i.e., sales revenue minus all expenses except, of course, the cost of Shareowners' equity. In the context of the P/E and PEG ratios, the E is earnings per share, or EPS.*
Earnings Guidance:	*Earnings guidance represents an insider's view of expected future sales or earnings, which is given to analysts or to the market.*
Earnings per Share (EPS):	*Earnings per share is essentially the net income of the company divided by the number of outstanding shares.*
Enterprise Value:	*Enterprise Value is the key benchmark of a company's value. Enterprise Value is the current value of all of the cash that is or will be in the company, and which can be returned to Shareowners.*
	More specifically, it includes three items: (1) the current cash in the company, (2) MINUS the company's current debt. (current debt is subtracted because cash must be used to pay off the debt.), (3) PLUS the present value of all the cash flow that the company will have in the future which can be returned to Shareowners. The present value of this future cash flow is calculated by forecasting the company's free cash flow and discounting it to the present value using the company's weighted average cost of capital (WACC).

Financial Markets:	The term "financial markets" usually includes capital markets plus trading in derivative instruments, commodities, and foreign exchange. It is a much more encompassing term than "capital markets," although both of them include markets in which, at some point, cash is exchanged rather than physical goods.
GAAP (Pronounced "gap"):	See Generally Accepted Accounting Principles.
Generally Accepted Accounting Principles (or GAAP):	GAAP is a set of accounting principles that have been formally codified by various accounting bodies since the middle of the twentieth century. Because there is conflict between some of these codifications, a hierarchy of four categories of accounting principles has been established to help resolve conflicts. In the event that conflict still exists, GAAP leaves it up to the individual accountant or auditor to use the principle that best reflects the substance of the transaction.
	Conclusion: GAAP is a human attempt at a political compromise on a measurement model. It is not a science.
Growth (G):	In the context of a company and the creation of Shareowner Value, growth means increasing the company's Enterprise Value.
	In the context of the PEG ratio, growth is the growth rate (G) of a company's free cash flow. Generally, that growth should be the anticipated growth over the next three to five years.
Investment Analysts:	Investment analysts are individuals who examine the business and financials of a company in order to forecast its prospects and stock value.

Investment Bank:

An investment bank is an entrepreneurial organization that either invests its own money in stocks or bonds (including venture capital) or offers to be the intermediary or insurer (underwriter) of the placement and pricing of new issues of debt and equity, either in the public or private markets. They also work with legal, tax and accounting advisors to find ways to arbitrage, or "get around," capital market, tax, and accounting barriers standing in the way of something that a company is trying to achieve. Usually company management is trying to increase earnings per share (EPS). A major business is in acting as advisors or "marriage brokers" in acquisitions and divestitures.

Investment Bankers:

Individuals who work for the investment banks.

Market Value:

The Market Value of a company is the total dollar value of the Shareowner's current investment in the company based upon the market value of the stock. In general it is computed as follows:

Market Value = Share Price x Number of Outstanding Shares.

For example: If the Share Price = $150, and the Number of Outstanding Shares = 10,000,000, then the Market Value of the company is $1,500,000,000 ($1.5 billion).

Price (P):

Price (P) is the price of a share of stock.

Price-to-Earnings (P/E) Ratio or P/E Multiple:

The price-to-earnings ratio and the P/E multiple are the same thing. They are the ratio of the stock price (P) to the earnings per share (E or EPS).

For example, if the stock price is $15 and earnings per share is $1, then the P/E multiple is 15 (15/1). This is sometimes abbreviated to say that the "P/E" or "P/E ratio" is 15.

Peg Ratio (PEG):

The PEG ratio is the company's P/E ratio divided by the growth (G) rate of its free cash flow.

Sarbanes-Oxley Act: *The Sarbanes-Oxley Act of 2002 was the Congressional reaction to the crisis in corporate responsibility. It was an eclectic set of measures designed to increase corporate accountability for GAAP reporting, increased regulatory authority for enforcing reporting standards, and increased criminal penalties for fraud. It also provides new supervision of public auditors by the Securities and Exchange Commission through the Public Company Accounting Oversight Board.*

S.E.C.: *Securities and Exchange Commission. The federal regulatory body having responsibility for regulating issuers in public financial markets in the United States.*

Shareowner: *The Shareowner is the person who has worked hard to accumulate savings. S/he then lets others use that cash to earn a fair living by creating products and services. The Shareowner only expects to receive his investment back with a fair return.*

Valuation Statement: *The Valuation Statement is a proposed fourth public audited financial statement (in addition to the income statement, balance sheet, and cash flow). The Valuation Statement provides a calculation of the "no-growth" Enterprise Value of a company as well as a sensitivity analysis of the Enterprise Value under several growth scenarios. Management would indicate and justify its expected growth rate, and then the free markets could decide what growth rate and which financial statement best served Shareowners.*

Please see the Appendix for a description and format.

Wall Street or Wall Street Firms: *"Wall Street" or "Wall Street firms" is used to mean all firms, regardless of geographic location, which perform investment banking and brokerage services. Today, this includes many large commercial banks.*

APPENDIX A

The Valuation Statement

The idea of the Valuation Statement is to provide investors with a fourth audited financial statement (in addition to the income statement, balance sheet, and cash flow). The Valuation Statement would provide a calculation of the "no-growth" Enterprise Value of a company as well as a sensitivity analysis of the Enterprise Value under several growth scenarios. Management would indicate and justify its expected growth rate, and then the free markets could decide what growth rate and which financial statement(s) best served Shareowners.

The following excerpt is from the author's book Rich Shareowner, Poor Shareowner, *and defines the Valuation Statement. The conversation takes place in the evening around a campfire on a cattle drive in the high San Juan Mountains of Colorado. Characters who speak in the chapter include:*

Ranch Hands:

Terry Brandon	Trail Cook	Illinois
Sean Lone Eagle	Trail Scout	South Dakota
Sam McAllen	Chief Host & Trail Boss	Midwest

Guests:

Wendy Stevens	Searcher and Investment Banker	New York, NY
Debra & John Morgan	Debra: Professor, Northwestern University School of Business; John: Attorney Children: Nicholas	Evanston, Il
Nancy & Steve Patterson	Nancy: Chemical Engineer Steve: CFO of billion-dollar high-tech firm Children: Emma, Fletcher	Boston, Mass.
Susan & Ed Rogers	Susan: Manager, Environmental Protection Agency Ed: Equity Analyst for a major bank	Charlotte, S.C.
Georgia & Tom Roman	Husband & Wife long-distance truck driving team	Washington state.
Barb & Mitch Thompson	Barb: CEO, $5-billion public consumer-products company. Mitch: Vice President, Human Resources at another large consumer-products company.	Midwest

Rich Shareowner, Poor Shareowner
Chapter 32
The Prize...Who Will Wear the White Hat?

Sam took the time during the interlude of whistling, cheering, and good-natured hooting to pour some coffee for everyone and to pass around the oatmeal-raisin cookies. He took several. He loved oatmeal-raisin cookies, and Terry made the best.

"So, Sam," said Wendy, "who's going to wear the White Hat?"

"It would just be speculation," said Sam, "but my guess is that *it will be worn by whoever has the most to gain.*"

That drew even more hoots and comments, such as, "It won't be you," as Sam laughed and choked on his coffee.

Nancy gave him a few "helpful" hard pats on the back, playfully twisted his ear, and, like a scolding sister, mercilessly said, "*Answer the question.*"

Slowly, Sam regained his cowboy composure, then lost it, then regained it, then continued, "There is a lot to be gained here. Money? Yes. But also political advantage, bureaucratic prestige, capital market liquidity, public interest, possibly national economic leadership, and yes, even pride and integrity. *There is a lot to be lost* as well. Money, political opportunity, bureaucratic influence, liquidity in national capital markets, national economic leadership, and even pride and integrity."

Sam continued, *"I surely hope the accountants will take the lead. For centuries, their role has been to provide creditors and Shareowners with an impartial valuation of their respective interests in the company.* While the valuation has been imperfect, it was at least credible within reason. As we just discussed, when the world moved slower, the income statement, cash flow, and balance sheet served yeoman's duty for the interests of both creditors and Shareowners. However, with the development of efficient financial markets, advances in financial theory and information technology, and the faster rate of change in the world today, these three statements no longer adequately serve Shareowners. There needs to be a fourth statement, a 'Valuation Statement,' that calculates Economic Profit and tells Shareowners how the company is doing relative to WACC—the weighted average cost of capital."

"After listening to Steve's earlier comments on the potential for conflicts and lost fees, *why would the accountants do it?"* asked Ed.

"Pride, and because it's their job," said Sam. "It may seem naive, but somewhere, some accountants must feel loyalty to their profession and a personal responsibility to ensure its future credibility with the public—to 'ride for the brand'—so to speak. *It is unmistakably clear that the three existing financial statements are increasingly misleading when it comes to Shareowners.* Reasonable and accurate disclosures of economic profit and issues surrounding Enterprise Value in a new GAAP Valuation Statement would go a long way to restoring public confidence."

"But if the accountants don't respond, who else could do it, besides them?" asked Debra.

Sam said, "By themselves, probably only the Securities and Exchange Commission, and that would essentially only be with respect to companies who issue debt or equity to the public."

"But," said Barb, "I am sure that there must be a lot of others who could collectively influence or cause a Valuation Statement to happen."

"You're right," said Sam. "People like equity analysts, bankers, directors, and even management could influence creation of a Valuation Statement. But let me focus on the most important, *Shareowners, who have the most to lose.* They can do a lot to influence, but like anything worthwhile, it will take work. To be successful, Shareowners will need to coordinate with each other. Here are some thoughts on what Shareowners can do:

- Shareowners can require their broker's equity analysts to prepare company Valuation Statements for them before they invest. Otherwise, Shareowners might as well use discount brokers or index funds.

- Shareowners can ask company management in writing and at Shareowner meetings to present a Valuation Statement.

- Shareowners can write to the Financial Standards Accounting Board (FASB) and the Securities and Exchange Commission, sending a copy to the external auditors and CEO/CFO at the companies they own. Their letter should request development of a new Valuation Statement and suggest contents.

- Institutional Shareowners, such as mutual funds, and Individual Shareowner clubs and organizations can act together to put in front of company directors resolutions that require incentive plans, including stock option grants, to be based upon creation of Economic Profit as a proxy for Enterprise Value. *The resolution should also require annual presentation of an Acquisition Valuation Statement for the company before any acquisition is made which is greater than fifteen percent of the size of the company.*

- Shareowners can write to the chairman and directors of the Federal Reserve and the major stock exchanges suggesting the importance of a Valuation Statement to the credibility, liquidity, and continued global leadership of U.S. financial markets.

- Shareowners can write to the President, representatives, and senators in Congress advocating the importance of a Valuation Statement to the credibility, liquidity, and global leadership of our financial markets as well. They must also stress the efficient use of resources, especially people. Point out to the elected representatives that *managing our companies based upon creation of Enterprise Value,* using economic profit as a proxy, *is an issue of national competitiveness. Whichever nation makes its management processes more effective is going to have a national competitive advantage, just as we saw from the Quality Process in the 1980s and 1990s. In this sense, society has the most to win or lose.* Some nation will be the leader, and the rest will play a very tough game of catch up."

In a puzzled voice, Tom asked, "What can government do?"

"Two things immediately come to mind," replied Sam. "First, the Commerce Department can create a prestigious national competitive award similar to the Baldridge Quality Award. The new award would recognize continuous creation of Economic Profit over a three-to five-year period. In addition, while I am not an advocate of the second idea, it would work and might have merit in an emergency. If the government really wanted to accelerate efficient use of society's resources, it could give tax incentives for increasing Economic Profit over a three-year period. This would accelerate the transition to Economic Profit based measurements throughout the economy."

Mitch picked up on Sam's observations. "Your comment about competitive advantage going to the early adopter nation obviously applies equally to companies. Shouldn't it be in management's self-interest to be first to implement Economic Profit-based incentive plans? If management waits until they see a competitor adopt it, they may have given the competition a two-year head start. That's hard to make up."

"Yes," said Sam. "In theory, companies should want to be the early adopter of Economic Profit-based incentive plans. However, because so many incentive plans are based upon accounting measures such as EPS and net income, management and Shareowner interests are only loosely aligned. Management wants the option of managing (arbitraging) the accounting rules in order to earn incentives, even though no Enterprise Value is created. It will take leadership, character, and real courage for management to initiate a change to Economic Profit-based plans, which demand creation of real cash value to get a payout."

Mitch nodded thoughtfully. "I understand your point, and unfortunately, I believe that you are right. It's hard for people to walk away from low-hanging fruit, even though it doesn't rightly belong to them."

There was an awkward pause in the conversation. Finally, Barb came to the rescue.

"I think the idea of a national award for creating Economic Profit is a wonderful idea," she said. "The award provides recognition, a standard measure of Economic Profit, and the winners can serve as benchmarks for others. I just hope that the application will be a lot simpler than the one for the Baldridge Quality Award."

"I like the idea too," said Steve.

"Back to earth, boys and girls," chided Wendy. "Whether it's used by Shareowners for the mundane purpose of investing, or," she good-naturedly mocked, "by the President for a prestigious national award, what should a Valuation Statement contain?"

Sam knew that her sarcasm was directed at him. He threw his hands in the air and with a laugh said, "Okay, okay, I surrender. But remember, 'Without vision, the people perish.'"

His eyes twinkled as he smiled at Wendy, and he continued, "Let's focus on the contents of a GAAP Valuation Statement for Shareowners. I am sure that the President can design his own valuation statement for the national award."

As he spoke, he reached for his saddlebags and to everyone's surprise pulled out a pack of laminated pages. "I have been boiling this down for quite a while, and this laminate represents my current thinking on the subject."

As he passed out the laminates, Sam continued, "This laminate presents a basic Valuation Statement. It is intended to be simple and understandable, and to capture ninety-five percent of the value with five percent of the effort. Remember that the intent of the Valuation Statement is to show the trend in Economic Profit computed from the simple formula we discussed earlier this week. Also, remember, the company doesn't necessarily have to have a positive Economic Profit (EP) in any given year, as long as the trend is strongly toward a positive EP over, say, a three-year period."

$$\text{Economic Profit or (EP)} = \text{Net Operating Profit after Tax (NOPAT)*} - \text{Capital} \times \text{WACC}$$

* plus material non-cash items such as goodwill amortization

As flashlights were turned on, Sam pointed to the top part of the sheet and slowly moved down the different categories, commenting on the highlights of each topic:

- **'Cash Basis' NOPAT:** "'Cash Basis' NOPAT is a misnomer. We are not trying to restate the income statement to pure cash accounting. All we want to do is to add back the material non-cash items so that we get as close as possible to the cash income coming in the door. For example, we add back expense related to amortization of goodwill because it is a non-cash expense. We do not add back depreciation, because cash related to it is typically reinvested in replacement assets; however, this should be revisited depending on the company and as conditions change. We add back rents because they are a form of financial expense that will be addressed through the mechanism of adding back the off balance sheet lease assets to capital. Observe where NOPAT fits in the EP equation above."

"How would you handle 'one-time' events, such as non-recurring gains or charges?" asked Debra.

"The GAAP accounting charge related to these items would be excluded from the 'Cash Basis' NOPAT calculation," said Sam. "However, any cash from the gain or any cash cost associated with the charge would be added to, or subtracted from, the 'Cash Basis' NOPAT on a separate line. The reason is that the cash does create (or destroy) value even if it is only one time. By putting it on a separate line, a Shareowner can still see the trend in the ongoing business."

- **Capital:** "The 'Capital' section identifies all of the capital (debt plus equity) used in the business regardless of whether it is on the balance sheet or not. The company would be required to identify the capital it is using in the form of financing, operating, and synthetic leases as well as those sourced through any other off-balance sheet method, such as receivable discounting or asset securitization. *'On' or 'Off'-balance sheet financing structure is NOT the criteria for including capital related to an asset in the definition of capital. The criterion is whether the asset continues to be used in the business.* Observe where capital fits into the EP equation."

- **Cost of Capital:** "The 'Cost of Capital' section computes the WACC (weighted average cost of capital). To do that, the company must reveal the cost of each category of capital. For debt, the company would use the actual weighted debt cost after tax. The tax rate would be the combined statutory tax rate. For the cost of equity, the company would use the past twelve months U.S. inflation rate plus eight percent. This cost and methodology would be defined by the accounting standard establishing the Valuation Statement. The standard should be based upon what a broad market index earns. It would be based upon the premise that any individual equity must at least earn the long term, historical risk premium of the market to inflation. Otherwise, investors should just buy an S&P 500 index fund. I would not use betas. Setting a pragmatic standard is the most critical issue at this point. Observe where the WACC fits into the Economic Profit equation."

- **Economic Profit:** "The Economic Profit reveals in dollar terms how much value is being created (or destroyed) in the current year, i.e., how many dollars of 'Cash Basis NOPAT' it is earning above or below its Cost of Capital. *It tells the Shareowner in dollar terms how much Economic Profit is being created (or destroyed)."*

- **Net Economic Return on Capital:** "The Net Economic Return on Capital (NEROC) reveals in percent terms how much value is being created or destroyed in a given year. It compares the rate of return earned in a given year to the WACC for that year. *It tells a Shareowner in percent terms how much more or less the board is earning on the company's investments than the cost of the money that the company is investing.* If NEROC is not equal to WACC, the Enterprise Value will decrease. NEROC is a macro indicator for the company and should not be used to manage business units within the company. Economic Profit accomplishes that task much more effectively. The one-line EP formula is much easier for front-line people to operationalize than ratios like ROCE and NEROC."

- **Financial Goals:** "The Financial Goals section requires management to state their current financial goals so that Shareowners can see what goals management is targeting and the amount of increase being targeted for each goal."

- **Incentive Plan Design:** "The section on Incentive Plan Design reveals, by management layer, the types and structures of the incentive plans in which they participate, including basis of payment and amount paid in relationship to Economic Profit created. It also provides Shareowners with the expected incentive payout for each of the top five officers in relation to increases in Economic Profit per share and the market value per share over the incentive time period."

"Wow," said Debra, "this Valuation Statement really provides some useful information. As I look at it, *I think that a useful addition would be a computation of the Enterprise Value, assuming that the Economic Profit has not changed."*

"How would you do that?" asked Tom.

Debra said, "Enterprise Value is equal to the beginning capital plus the present value of EP discounted at the WACC."

She continued, "We know the capital at the end of the year, the WACC, and the Economic Profit. If EP does not change (i.e., a no-growth scenario) then the present value of Economic Profit is merely the current Economic Profit divided by the WACC. *In other words, we capitalize the Economic Profit at the WACC.* Let me show you an example. Assume that capital was $1 billion, that WACC was nine percent, and that Economic Profit was $50mm. We could calculate a No-Growth Enterprise Value as follows":

'NO-GROWTH' ENTERPRISE VALUE

	Year 1
Capital at Year End:	$1,000
Plus: Economic Profit divided by WACC	$555
No-Growth Enterprise Value:	**$1,555**

"Debra," asked Steve, "how do you use this? Doesn't this understate the Enterprise Value for most companies?"

"Yes." said Debra, "because most companies have growth, this will understate Enterprise Value. However, *it serves as a factual, rational data point for what the company is worth, assuming no growth. It also serves as a benchmark from which management can discuss their expectations for growth in Enterprise Value.* The Valuation Statement can also be amplified to include a sensitivity-analysis table, showing constant growth rates through year ten and the resultant Enterprise Value, as well as management's comments on their expected growth of Economic Profit and change in Enterprise Value. Shareowners can then compare this chart and management's expectations to the implicit growth rate contained in the company's market P/E ratio."

"Let's add it to the Valuation Statement for now," recommended Steve. "I agree with Debra that it is a quantifiable, supportable, and rational starting point to get people thinking about Enterprise Value."

"Done," said Sam.

Georgia then said, "I notice that the back of the laminate contains a sheet called *Acquisition Valuation Statement.* What is it?"

Sam responded, "As we discussed earlier this week, acquisitions are major events in the life of a company; seventy percent of the time, they destroy Enterprise Value. We need a way to make boards and management visibly accountable for acquisitions, without necessarily revealing purchase price and other confidential information. This Acquisition Valuation Statement *represents an attempt at giving the Shareowners the information they need in order to ensure that the boards and management are acting responsibly in the Shareowners' interests.* It can be presented whenever a company acquires another company that is at least fifteen percent of the size of the acquirer."

"Please explain it to us?" asked John.

"Glad to," said Sam. "The Acquisition Valuation Statement asks the acquirer to report only two things. The first is the acquisition's pro-forma *incremental* impact on Economic Profit for each of the next five calendar years, beginning with the pro-rata impact in the year of acquisition. This calculation includes all 'synergies' the acquirer expects to achieve anywhere in the consolidated acquirer. The capital used in the calculation includes the purchase price plus assumed debt (including off-balance sheet debt) at a cost equal to the acquirer's WACC."

Sam continued, "The second item the acquirer must report is the net present value of the acquired company, including synergies, or the net present value of the Enhanced Cash Flows. The discount rate used in this calculation is the acquirer's WACC. The acquirer presents this statement at the time of acquisition as well as in its annual report. Notice that we are using the acquirer's pre-acquisition WACC, as opposed to post-acquisition WACC, as it is usually a more conservative (i.e., higher) discount rate at a point in time, and using it also prevents speculation on how the acquisition will be financed."

"That's pretty good," said Wendy. "You get to see the best of both worlds and management doesn't have to reveal the purchase price, the assumed growth rates, or synergies if they are sensitive to the seller or for competitive reasons. The NPV of the acquired company tells Shareowners how much the acquirer's Enterprise Value will increase (or decrease) if plans go as advertised. That calculation is, of course, based on a long-term forecast, and *I assume that the accounting standard for the Acquisition Valuation Statement would define a standard annuity formula with no growth after year ten and calculated using the cash flow in year-ten divided by the WACC.* The other part I like is that the Economic Profit calculations in the first five years give Shareowners a sense that the returns will be realized beginning now. That helps to reduce the risk that the acquisition's returns will depend on, achieving a hockey-stick forecast in years five through ten."

"It looks good to me, and I can understand it," said Georgia.

Sam replied, "Glad you see the sense in it."

He continued, "If I were really defining the Valuation and Acquisition Valuation Statements, I would assemble a small group of CFOs, Economic Profit consultants, and compensation specialists, accountants, and equity analysts, among others, to propose the statements' contents. The group would include people with real-world experience in managing companies and in measuring and motivating people to efficiently create Enterprise Value. That way, the statement design would have a better chance of motivating creation of Enterprise Value while preventing, or at least minimizing, the prospects of people 'gaming' the system."

"Hey, Sam," said Georgia. "Who's going to wear the 'White Hat' and ride Silver?"

"It won't be me," replied Sam. "I ride an Appaloosa named War Bonnet."

They all laughed, and in the silence that followed, the melody and words of the song 'Home on the Range' drifted over from the larger campfire. Flashlights were extinguished, and Sam's contingent relaxed against their saddles and gazed at the sky, watching sparks from the fire drift to the heavens while enjoying the serenade.

Valuation Statement

'CASH-BASIS NOPAT'

	Year 1	Year 2	Year 3
Operating Profit Before Tax (from income statement):			
Plus Amortization of goodwill:			
Plus Rents:			
Minus Statutory Tax Rate*:			
Plus (*or minus*) After-tax CASH impact of one-time gains (*or charges*) not included in operating profit before taxes:			
'Cash-Basis NOPAT':			

*The combined federal, state, and local statutory tax rate in the U.S. is about 38%, assuming full absorption of excess foreign tax credits.

CAPITAL:

		End of Year:		
	Year 0	Year 1	Year 2	Year 3
Debt:				
Short Term:				
Long Term:				
Off Balance Sheet, including asset securitizations, operating, financial and synthetic leases:				
Total Debt:				
Average Debt Capital:	N/A			
Total Equity (Based Upon Market Value):				
Average Equity Capital:	N/A			
Total Capital:				
Average Total Capital:	N/A			

COST OF CAPITAL*:

	Year 1	Year 2	Year 3
Cost of Debt, After Tax:			
Short Term:			
Long Term:			
Off Balance Sheet, including asset securitizations, operating, financial and synthetic leases:			
Weighted Average Cost of Debt (After Tax):			
Cost of Equity (After Tax using the calendar year Consumer Price Index plus 8% as the after-tax cost):			
Weighted Average Cost of Capital (Using average debt and average market value of equity):			

*All amounts after tax at statutory tax rate in Cash-Basis NOPAT calculation

ECONOMIC PROFIT:

	Year 1	Year 2	Year 3
Cash-Basis NOPAT:			
Minus **Average Capital x WACC:**			
Economic Profit:			

NET ECONOMIC RETURN ON CAPITAL (NEROC):

	Year 1	Year 2	Year 3
Cash-Basis NOPAT:			
Divided by **Average Capital:**			
Economic Return on Capital:			
Minus **WACC:**			
Net Economic Return on Capital			

MARKET VALUE:

	End of Year:		
	Year 1	Year 2	Year 3
Share Price:			
Multiplied by **Outstanding Shares:**			
Market Value:			

NO-GROWTH ENTERPRISE VALUE:

	End of Year:		
	Year 1	Year 2	Year 3
Capital at Year End:			
Plus **Economic Profit** *divided by* **WACC:**			
No-Growth Enterprise Value:			

ENTERPRISE VALUE SENSITIVITY AND OUTLOOK:

Provide a sensitivity-analysis table showing growth rates through year ten and the resultant Enterprise Value as well as management's comments on their expected growth rates and change in Enterprise Value.

FINANCIAL GOALS:

Provide a brief description of management's current financial goals and the rate of change anticipated in them. For example: our goal is to increase Economic Profit fifty percent p.a. over the next five years and twenty-five percent p.a. thereafter through year ten.

INCENTIVE PLAN DESIGN:

Provide a description of incentive plans, revealing, by management layer, the types and structures of the incentive plans in which different groups of managers participate, including basis of payment and amount paid in relationship to Economic Profit created. The section also provides Shareowners with the expected incentive payout for each of the top five officers in relation to increases in Economic Profit per share and the market value per share over the incentive time period.

Acquisition Valuation Statement

Proforma Impact on Economic Profit:

	Year 1	Year 2	Year 3	Year 4	Year 5
Incremental Economic Profit					

This represents the board's estimate of the increase in the acquirer's Economic Profit resulting from the acquisition in each of the first five years. It is based upon the concept of Enhanced Cash Flow, and therefore includes projected "synergies."

Net Present Value of Acquisition:

This represents the board's estimate of the increase in the acquirer's Enterprise Value resulting from the acquisition, assuming no growth in the acquired company subsequent to the tenth year, and after subtracting the purchase price, including assumed debt. The acquirers' current WACC is used as the discount rate. The notes here would explain the assumed growth rate, margin, synergies, and WACC used in the calculations.

APPENDIX B

Wendy's Notes

*During her meetings with Sam McAllen, Sean Lone Eagle, and Georgia Roman,
Wendy took notes on selected topics so that she would be sure she had information to
share with her friends. This is a copy of her notes.*

Distractions: Who to trust? What to believe?

1. Overcoming fear and extremes in the stock market involves three elements:

    1) Learning to recognize a 'fair' stock valuation
    2) Learning to recognize and ignore the distractions
    3) Disciplining yourself to invest using 1) and 2)

2. Knowledgeable investors understand the motivation of people around their money.

    Free enterprise is a process in which each individual acts in his own self interest, and in the process, creates value for society. Acting in one's self-interest is fundamental to our society. Every adult, and especially every Shareowner, should expect it of others and act accordingly. After all, the Shareowner himself is acting in his own self-interest, and in the process, his capital creates products and jobs that people need and want.

    Investors need to accept this reality and deal with it.

    Knowledgeable investors deal with it before the fact (i.e., before they invest) because they know that after the fact, even an army of lawyers can't recover enough to compensate all the plaintiffs of a bankrupt or restructured company.

3. There are two general guidelines when it comes to understanding the motivation of people around your money.

    One: You must assume that everyone is acting in his own self-interest.

    Two: You can usually predict what a person will do and what his self-interest is if you can identify how he or she and their company are measured and paid.

4. Investors must discipline themselves to ignore the distractions and to invest based upon the real value, the Enterprise Value, of a company. They must stop investing based on the assumption that there will always be someone else, 'a Greater Fool,' to bail them out at a higher stock price.

5. The Grand Deception and the root cause of the crisis in corporate responsibility is a measurement system that considers Shareowners' equity to be free. The implication is that the Shareowner has no required return and will be satisfied with whatever is left over after all other costs have been paid.

Enterprise Value, Stock Price, and the Quick Fix

ENTERPRISE VALUE:

Enterprise Value represents the present value of all of the cash flow that a company has or will have. It uses the investor's desired benchmark yield as the discount rate. A reasonable benchmark is the return on the S&P 500 stock index, which has earned inflation plus eight percent p.a. compounded over the past seventy years.

Enterprise Value	=	Current Cash	−	Current Debt	+	Present Value of All Future Free Cash Flow (Includes Growth)

The equation says that the Enterprise Value of a company equals—

1. the cash held in bank accounts or liquid investments, MINUS

2. the cash required to pay off *all* of its borrowed debt, PLUS

3. the current (present) value of all the cash that it will generate in the future and that it can return to Shareowners without impairing growth.

THE TWO CASH VALUES OF A COMPANY:

Cash is society's store of value. A company has two cash values: its stock price and its Enterprise Value.

THE RELATIONSHIP OF STOCK PRICE AND ENTERPRISE VALUE:

The Theory: In theory, what could be more logical than to say that the market value of a company (its stock price times the number of shares outstanding) should equal the Enterprise Value (the present value of the cash inside the company)?

Stock Price	**=**	**Enterprise Value Per Share**

The Reality: The reality is that the stock price and Enterprise Value are almost never equal. The 2nd Most Powerful Formula in Finance explains who and how value is created for Shareowners. In the process, it provides individual investors with insight on how to earn their benchmark return.

| Stock Price | = | Enterprise Value Per Share | + | Supply & Demand for the Stock |

Creation of Shareowner Value: Management vs. Shareowner	Responsibility of Management	Responsibility of Individual Shareowners
The Shareowner's return is earned by the difference between the price at which he buys and sells the stock, plus dividends.	Management controls the creation or destruction of free cash flow in a company as well as the company's cost of capital. These are the two factors that create or destroy Enterprise Value.	Shareowners control the price at which they individually buy or sell a stock. The Shareowner's objective is to buy a stock below Enterprise Value and to sell at a stock price above Enterprise Value.
Rate of Change:	Enterprise Value changes slowly over time because it is driven by changes in free cash flow resulting from the company's operations.	Supply and demand is volatile because many transient events, ranging from company- or industry-specific to world events, affect it.
Stock Analysis: Fundamental vs. Technical	Fundamental Analysis	Technical Analysis
	In stock investing, calculating the Enterprise Value using research into cash flows and expected growth rates is known as fundamental analysis.	In stock investing, assessing the price and volume movements of a stock while investing is known as technical analysis.
Stock Price Movement	Fifty Percent of the Stock Price Movement	Fifty Percent of the Stock Price Movement
	Data shows that at least fifty percent of stock price movement is correlated with changes in Economic Profit, a proxy for Enterprise Value.	The implication is that fifty percent of stock price movement is due to various supply & demand factors.

Value Creation vs. Wealth Transfer	Creates Economic Value	Transfers Economic Value
	Earning more than the cost of capital reflects a company that is using capital effectively, and therefore is creating economic value for society.	Other than the liquidity value, transferring wealth between people creates no new economic value for society.

THE INVESTOR'S GOAL:

In order to increase the probability of earning his benchmark return of inflation plus eight percent, an investor should try to buy a stock when its price is below the Enterprise Value and to sell it when its price is above its Enterprise Value. The price/earnings-to-growth (PEG) ratio described below provides a "quick fix" that enables investors to do it.

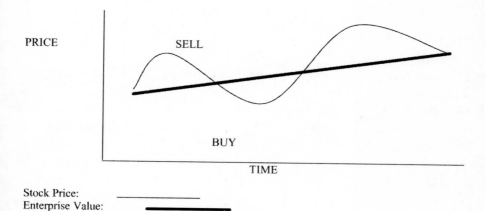

Stock Price: _____
Enterprise Value: ▬▬▬▬▬▬

PEG RATIOS
For 10% yield

(1)	(2)	(3)	P/E / G Ratio (4)	Reality Check Column (5)
Current P/E (Price/ Earnings)	Pay Me Now, Current Yield to Shareowners Implied by Current P/E	Or Pay Me Later, Minimum Annual Growth Rate for 10 Years (% p.a.) Required to Justify P/E by Making Up Current Yield Shortfall.	BUT PAY ME! Maximum Price/Earnings to Growth Rate ('PEG') Ratio Required to Earn 10%	Size of Company Sales in 10 Years If Grown at Minimum Annual Growth Rate. (Starting from $1mm.)
10	10%	0%	-	$1.0
13	7.7	5	2.6	1.6
17	5.9	10	1.7	2.6
21	4.8	15	1.4	4.0
28	3.6	20	1.4	6.2
38	2.6	25	1.5	9.3
51	2.0	30	1.7	13.8
68	1.5	35	1.9	20.1
92	1.1	40	2.3	28.9
122	0.8	45	2.7	41.1
163	0.6	50	3.3	57.7

This model assumes a constant growth rate of Annual Cash Flow for ten years and no growth thereafter.
This is reasonable, because most companies will need major capital or research investment by the tenth year in order to extend the growth curve. ACQUIITIONS DO NOT COUNT IN ADDING GROWTH. In most cases, the acquirer pays away the value of acquired cash flows and synergies in the purchase price.

The first column is the current P/E ratio.

The second column is the current yield to the Shareowner implied by the current P/E ratio.

The third column shows the implied compound growth rate of Annual Cash Flow associated with a given P/E. It also represents the minimum growth rate required to make up the current shortfall in yield versus the Shareowner's target yield of 10%.

Column four is the PEG ratio. It shows the maximum Price-to-Earnings ratio that a Shareowner would pay for the growth in the third column if he wanted to earn 10% (i.e., The PEG ratio is the P/E divided by Growth).

Column five is a reality check! It shows in dollar terms how big the company's sales would be at the end of ten years if it grew at the implied annual growth rate.

Because of inefficiencies in projecting future growth and in the correlation of GAAP earnings to cash flow, many investors limit their purchases to stocks with a PEG ratio of 1 or less.

The National Solution

The national failure in corporate governance is the failure of Generally Accepted Accounting Principles to measure the creation (or destruction) of economic value (Enterprise Value) in companies. The national solution is to incorporate a Valuation Statement into Generally Accepted Accounting Principles (GAAP), which includes the current cost of Shareowners' equity as a cost of doing business.

About the Author

Will Marshall has over twenty-seven years experience in corporate finance and as a corporate officer. Will began his career in international banking and worked in the Seoul, Korea, branch of The First National Bank of Chicago (now Bank One). In 2000, he retired as Treasurer of Nalco Chemical Company, a $2.5-billion global water-treatment company. Upon becoming Nalco's treasurer at age thirty-four, he built and managed a world-class global treasury operation for over twenty years. He served on the boards of a number of Nalco's international subsidiaries, including those in India, Saudi Arabia, and Canada. He has been invited to speak on financial topics at insurance and business forums in addition to training Nalco's managers worldwide.

Will and his wife, Bev, built, own, and operate The Meadows Farm Ltd., a hunter/jumper and dressage training facility in Hawthorn Woods, Illinois. Bev and Will are active supporters of the University of Illinois Equestrian Team.

Will is a 1968 graduate of Lehigh University, with a BS in Industrial Engineering, *cum laude*. He did two years of graduate work at the Wharton Graduate School of the University of Pennsylvania. In 1985, he completed the Advanced Management Program at Harvard Business School.

From 1970–1974, Will served as a lieutenant, Naval Flight Officer, and Mission Commander in the U.S. Navy.

Will is an Eagle Scout, and in 1999 was named a Distinguished Eagle Scout. He has been active in a number of leadership positions in scouting.

Will is an Associate Member of the Western Writers of America.

In 2002, Will's first book, *Rich Shareowner, Poor Shareowner!*, was published. The *Stock Trader's Almanac:2003* named it to their list of the "Year's Top Investment Books."

The author can be contacted through his website at www.will-marshall.com.

Bibliography

- Einstein, Albert. *Relativity: The Special and General Theory*. New York: Wings Books, 1961.

- Ehrbar, Al. *EVA: The Real Key to Creating Wealth*. New York: John Wiley & Sons, Inc., 1998.

- Hirsch, Yale, & Jeffret A. Hirsch. *Stock Trader's Almanac: 2003*. Old Tappan, N.J.: The Hirsch Organization Inc., 2002.

- Ibbotson Associates. *Stocks, Bonds, Bills and Inflation Yearbook*. Chicago: Ibbotson Associates, 2002.

- Marshall, Will. *Rich Shareowner, Poor Shareowner! Common Sense for Investors and Managers!* Lincoln: iUniverse, 2002.

- O'Neil, William J. *How to Make Money in Stocks: A Winning System in Good Times or Bad*, 3rd ed. New York: McGraw-Hill, 2002.

- Previts, Gary John and Barbara Dubis Merino. *A History of Accountancy in the United States: The Cultural Significance of Accounting*. Columbus: Ohio State University Press, 1998.

- Scherkenbach, William W. *The Deming Route to Quality and Productivity*. Washington, D.C.: Ceep Press, 1988.

- Smith, Adam. *The Wealth of Nations*. Chicago: Gateway, 1967 reprint.

- Stewart, G. Bennett, III. *The Quest for Value: The EVA™ Management Guide*. New York: Harper Business, 1994.

- Willaims, Jan R. *Miller GAAP Guide*. New York: Harcourt Professional Publishing, Year of Pub.

Endnotes

[1]. "Problems for Affluent Americans," *USA Today*, Business Section, 7 November 2002.

[2]. Wendy's vacation and the discussions at the ST Bar ranch are contained in the author's book *Rich Shareowner, Poor Shareowner!: Common Sense for Investors and Managers!*, Lincoln: iUniverse, 2002.

[3]. "More Earnings Restatements on the Way," *USA Today*, 25 October 2002.

"Sarbanes Releases Result of Probe into Proliferation of 'Restatements of Earnings' and Faulty Accounting Practices," *Press Release, U.S. Senate Committee on Banking, Housing and Urban Affairs*, 23 October 2002.

[4]. "Mutual Funds and IPO Bankers Danced Close," *The Wall Street Journal*, 12 March 2003.

[5]. "Fund Probe Turns to Walk Street," *The Wall Street Journal*, 10 September 2003.

[6]. "Imperfect Partners Most Merged Companies Trail Peers, Tribune Study Finds," Series: The Big Deals: Promises Unfulfilled, *The Chicago Tribune*, 18 March 2001.

"Mergers: Why Most Big Deals Don't Pay Off," *Business Week*, 14 October 2002.

[7]. "Left Out of Shrinking Research Pool, Companies Resort to Buying Coverage," *The Wall Street Journal*, 26 March 2003.

[8]. "Citicorp's Weill Might Avoid Charges over Faulty Research," *The Wall Street Journal*, 18 December 2002.

"Banking's Bigwigs May Be Beyond the Law's Reach," *Business Week,* 19 May 2003.

"Citicorp's Chairman is Barred from Direct Talks with Analysts," *The New York Times,* 29 April 2003.

[9]. "Latest Call on Wall Street: Get a Real Job," *The Wall Street Journal,* 28 February 2003. Of 3,800 Nasdaq Stock Market companies, 44% have no analysts covering them and another 14% have only one analyst following them.

[10]. "Analysts Repute as Stock Pickers under Challenge," *The New York Times,* 13 November 2002.

[11]. "Analysts Make Stock Calls, But Market Doesn't Listen," *Investor's Business Daily,* 15 September 2003.

[12]. Brendan Boyd, "Bankruptcies Don't Stop Companies' Positive Ratings," *Daily Herald,* 25 October 2002.

[13]. A Valuation Statement that calculates a company's Enterprise Value under a 'no-growth' scenario as well as provides a calculation of Enterprise Value under probable growth scenarios is presented in the Appendix.

[14]. "Imperfect Partners: Most Merged Companies Trail Peers, Tribune Study Finds," Series: The Big Deals: Promises Unfulfilled, *The Chicago Tribune,* 18 March 2001.

"Mergers: Why Most Big Deals Don't Pay Off," *Business Week,* 14 October 2002.

[15]. Margin requirements are the maximum amount of a stock's price, which can be borrowed using the stock as collateral.

[16]. Resigned, 5 November 2002: Harvey L. Pitt, Chairman, SEC; Resigned, 8 November 2002, Robert K. Herdman, Chief Accountant, SEC; Resigned, 12 November 2002, William H. Webster, newly-appointed chairman of the SEC's Public Company Accounting Oversight Board ("Oversight Board"). These resignations were the result of over six months of missteps by Pitt, culmi-

nating when he launched an SEC probe of himself and his nomination of Webster as chairman of the new Oversight Board. Pitt's resignation followed his action of withholding information from the SEC commissioners when they voted on Webster's nomination. The information was that Webster had headed the audit committee of U.S. Technologies when they fired the independent auditors after the auditors had cited "material weaknesses in the company's internal controls in a letter to the SEC." At the time of the nomination, Shareowners were in the process of suing the company for fraud—even though Webster himself was not accused of any wrongdoing. Herdman reportedly conducted the background check on Webster, and between Herdman and Pitt, the SEC's commissioners were not made aware of the potential problem in Webster's credentials. *The New York Times* and *The Wall Street Journal,* November, 2002.

[17]. "The Fall of Andersen: A Final Accounting' Series", *The Chicago Tribune*, September 1–4, 2002

[18]. "The Fall of Andersen: A Final Accounting' Series", *The Chicago Tribune*, September 1–4, 2002

[19]. See, for example, Gary John Previts and Barbara Dubis Merino, *A History of Accountancy in the United States* (Columbus: Ohio State University Press, 1998).

[20]. "Fiscal Officer Ousted at Auditor's Request," *The New York Times*, 15 February 2003.

[21]. "The Revolution That Wasn't :10 Years Later, Corporate Oversight Is Still Dismal," *The New York Times*, 26 January 2003.

[22]. Al Ehrbar, *EVA: The Real Key to Creating Wealth* (New York: John Wiley & Sons, Inc., 1998).

[23]. Ibbotson Associates, *Stocks, Bonds, Bills and Inflation Yearbook* (Chicago: Ibbotson Associates, 2002).

[24]. Will Marshall, *Rich Shareowner, Poor Shareowner!: Common Sense for Investors and Managers!* (Lincoln: iUniverse, 2002).

[25].   "Motorola's Profit: Special Again," *Wall Street Journal*, 15 October 2002.

[26].   "Is Your Job Next?," *Business Week*, 3 February 2003.

[27].   Albert Einstein, *Relativity: The Special and General Theory* (New York: Wings Books, 1961).

0-595-29778-1